SCREENPRINTING

SCREENPRINTING

JANE SAMPSON

ROBERT HALE

First published in 2017 by Robert Hale, an imprint of The Crowood Press Ltd,
Ramsbury, Marlborough, Wiltshire SN8 2HR

www.crowood.com

www.halebooks.com

British Library Cataloguing-in-Publication Data
A catalogue record for this book is available from the British Library.

ISBN 978 0 7198 1000 8

Title page image: *Dream Street*, silkscreen print by Jane Sampson.

Typeset and designed by D & N Publishing, Baydon, Wiltshire

Printed and bound in Malaysia by Times Offset (M) Sdn Bhd

CONTENTS

PREFACE

This is a practical 'how to do it' book written with artists, designers and enthusiastic amateurs in mind. It is based on many years of experience as a professional artist/printmaker with a long track record of exhibiting and also working as a teacher and lecturer in colleges, universities and in my own open-access studio, Inkspot Press.

The book uses an accessible step-by-step approach, with separate chapters illustrating everything from basic paper stencil techniques and simple handmade approaches that do not require sophisticated equipment, to the use of more complex photographic stencils. It also covers making colour separations by hand and on the computer. It aims to enlighten and inspire, giving people the confidence to have a go at this most versatile of print media and to develop their own style.

I would like to thank all of the artists who kindly allowed me to photograph them at work, or contributed their time and imagery to the book. These are: John Parkinson (Parky), Anthony Downey, Frances Quail, Annie Mendelow, Jack Nash, Jodie Tableporter, Rachel Brookes-Read and Anita Bernacka, plus Fox Fisher (who took many of the photographs), all of whom are regulars at Inkspot Press. And last but not least, I would like to thank my partner, the print wizard, Andy from Handprint, who helped with the last two chapters.

Jane Sampson

Jane Sampson is an award-winning artist/printmaker with a specialist knowledge of screenprinting. She has been printing for over thirty years and has experience in both commercial and artistic environments. She is well known as an enthusiastic and inspiring teacher. She works from her open-access studio, Inkspot Press, in Brighton, as a part-time lecturer at Brighton University and as a short-course tutor at Westdean College (the Edward James Foundation). As a practising artist she exhibits widely, both in the UK and abroad, and her work is held in many private and public collections.

CHAPTER 1

INTRODUCTION

What is screenprinting?

In essence, screenprinting is a sophisticated form of stencilling, in which the stencil is carried on a fabric mesh that is tightly stretched across a frame. The advantage of mounting a stencil on a screen is that the stencil can have its floating parts (like the middle of an 'o') held in place by the mesh, whereas a traditional stencil would need to have 'ties' or bridges to hold some of its elements in place.

It is also known as silkscreenprinting, because in its infancy as a commercial process at the beginning of the nineteenth century early pioneers used silk 'bolting' cloth as the stretched fabric. Likewise in Europe it is called *sérigraphie*, *serigrafica* or *siebdruck* (French, Spanish and German) from the Greek/Latin root *seri* for silk. Fine Art prints are sometimes known as serigraphs, particularly in America, rather than screenprints, as a way to distinguish these prints from their commercial counterparts.

Nowadays the mesh is not made of silk. It is usually made of specially woven monofilament polyester, although in some applications nylon or stainless-steel meshes are used. Modern meshes are not prone to rotting and stretching with wear like silk and can be reclaimed after use.

The screen frames can either be made of wood or metal (usually steel or aluminium) to which the mesh is firmly glued. The frames have to be strong enough to resist the tension of the tightly stretched fabric without bowing and also must be water-resistant so that they do not warp with constant cleaning and reclaiming. The days are gone when it was sufficient to stretch a screen by hand and staple the fabric to the frame. In the wider world, screenprinting is a high-tech industry with equally high-tech industries creating machinery and supplies to service it.

The stencil image is printed, using a squeegee, by forcing ink or dye through the open areas of the mesh on to the paper or fabric underneath. In the early days, metal blades were used, but as these would eventually tear the silk, they were replaced by rubber blades, which, in turn, would wear down and harden with age. Today, squeegees usually consist of a flexible, very durable, polyurethane blade clamped into a wooden or aluminium handle.

When printing, the empty stencil is first loaded with ink using the squeegee (the flood bar on an automated printing table). This is called the flood stroke. The ink in the screen is then printed down on to the print with another stroke of the squeegee (the pull). Preparation – the artwork, stencil making, ink mixing and colour matching – forms a huge part of the process and can be time-consuming. The actual printing is a relatively fast procedure.

The stencil itself can be made in many different ways, both low- and high-tech. Its main function is to block the mesh in the non-printing areas and prevent the printing ink from penetrating through on to the substrate below. It has to resist the action of the squeegee blade and the printing ink without breaking down.

At the low-tech end, simple temporary stencils can be made from thin cut paper, or can be painted directly on to the mesh with fluid, which, when dry, will be ink-resistant (screen filler or screen block). Some stencils are cut on a backing such as Profilm and adhered to the mesh with solvent or water. Others make use of a resist technique rather like batik.

All of the above hands-on, direct methods are still in use, particularly amongst artists, designers and hobbyists who want to make their own prints. It is possible to work using these methods without having access to complicated or expensive equipment or even a workshop. They are still popular because they can produce a particular aesthetic, or look, that is hard to create in any other way, even on a computer. There is a physicality about screenprints that is hard to fake with an inkjet printer.

These direct methods also mean that the artist incorporates his or her hand in the making process and can stay true to the immediacy of drawing, cutting or painting without any intervening mechanics. As such, screenprints are as satisfying to do, as they are absorbing and creative. While running my open-access print workshop and when teaching, I am constantly being told, particularly by graphic designers and Illustrators, just how much they enjoy 'getting their hands dirty' after long hours sitting at a computer screen. Also, the satisfaction of creating a product from start to finish simply cannot be matched.

However, by far the most reliable, accurate and widely used method of stencil making is photographic. Photo stencils are exposed on to the screen from a positive, using ultraviolet light. This allows an extraordinary array of textures, marks and imagery, whether hand-drawn or photographic, photocopied or computer-generated, to be used. This opens up a whole world of possibilities when it comes to image-making. Artists and designers have exploited this to great effect since the 1950s, although the technology to make photo stencils has actually been around since the turn of the nineteenth century.

A screen-printed image (graphic or Fine Art) is built up in layers of colour, one colour at a time. So, for example, if you were printing twenty two-colour prints on to paper using blue and black, you would first print all twenty sheets using the blue stencil. Then, when they were dry, you would print all twenty again using the black stencil. The black would have to print in the right place, registering with the blue, on every print, for the print run to work out successfully. To achieve this, a system of registration has to be used in multilayered, multicoloured designs.

Screenprinting is incredibly flexible when it comes to ink. The inks used can be mixed to different opacities (using transparent bases) and can be printed, either to cover a colour underneath or to let it show through, therefore creating a third colour (overprinting). The thickness of the layer of ink deposited can be controlled by using fine or coarse meshes. This makes it possible to print images on to an extraordinarily wide variety of surfaces and great vibrancy of colour can be achieved. Specialist inks, both solvent- and water-based, can be sourced to print on to paper or textiles, wood or vinyl, and also on to glass, ceramics, metal, plastic, rubber and polythene. There are ink mixtures that are scented, metallic, phosphorescent, fluorescent, heat-sensitive, electrically conductive or adhesive, or that carry glitter, mica, interference powders, or tiny reflective glass beads.

Since screenprinting is not, like etching or lithography, a pressure process, where an image is offset from a plate, it is possible to print on almost anything, even three-dimensional objects such as mugs or bottles or objects in situ, given the right equipment. It is simply one of the most versatile methods of printing in existence. Powered by commerce, over the years the process has been exploited and diversified by ingenious printers, technicians and entrepreneurs until there is hardly a consumer product that is not touched by it at some part of its manufacture.

If asked, most people would know that their T-shirts, caps, football shirts and other sports gear (basically anything that needs branding), their jackets, shirts and dresses, the fabric for their curtains, cushions and upholstery, tea towels, umbrellas, wallpaper, ceramic tiles, plates and mugs and so on are, more often then not, decorated using screenprinting. They might also realize that posters, banners and flags, stickers, billboards, display signage, estate-agent signs, road signs, car licence plates, skateboards, surf boards, beer mats, transfers, CDs and DVDs, bottles and containers of all kinds, are also screen-printed. As are the control panels and instrument panels on, for example, their washing machine or car dashboard.

But unless they were in the components trade, how many people would know that PCBs (printed circuit boards), semiconductors, biomedical sensors, fuel cells and membrane switches all use screenprinting as part of their manufacture and that its technical uses are constantly evolving?

Screenprinting is visible everywhere you look. Wherever there is a need for a cheap and controllable way of layering one substance on to another with extraordinary precision and endless repeatability, screenprinting will probably prove to be one of the simplest, most cost-effective ways of achieving it.

Given this extraordinary diversity and commercial success, the development of screenprinting as a medium for artistic expression is a drop in the ocean. But it is that significant drop that is the subject of this book. In the chapters that follow I will show you some of the inner secrets of screenprinting and explain just how you can explore and improve your techniques to produce fantastic prints.

CHAPTER 2

EQUIPMENT AND MATERIALS

Since this book is primarily aimed at artists, designers and those who would like to print their own work, my explanations cover flatbed printing and only mention commercial cylinder presses or rotary printing in passing.

Screen frames can be made of wood, aluminium or steel. DIY and very low-tech screenprinters use wooden screens, since almost any frame can be covered using organdie and a staple gun. Quite a few schools and colleges still do this for the sake of economy, mostly for printing on fabric. The screen can be stretched up in the same way as stretching a canvas, that is, starting in the middle of each side and working towards the corners, stapling as you go. A pair of canvas stretching pliers will make the job more efficient and will stretch the screen more tightly. Obviously the printed results that can be achieved through such a screen may be less than perfect, but perfection may not be the point when it is cheap, accessible and fun to do. There are plenty of 'out of the box' screen-printing kits that cater for the hobby end of the market.

Taken to the next level, wooden frames, even marine-ply ones, can sometimes warp out of shape after repeated reclaiming. They can also twist and lose tension, making registration difficult. Many T-shirt printers using a hand carousel will employ small wooden screens for repeat orders in cases where the screens are not going to be reclaimed afterwards and can eventually be regarded as expendable. It also makes a difference whether water- or oil-based inks are used. Many T-shirt printers use plastisol inks, which are washed down with mineral spirits rather than water. If wooden screens are repeatedly washed down with water, they are more likely to change shape.

Aluminium frames are the most reliable alternative in a small set-up, especially if you are intending to use people-friendly water-based inks. The frames can be recycled and recovered many times and will thus repay the extra cost. The larger the frame, the more likely it is that it will bow under the tension of the mesh. This will affect the registration of the print. For this reason, steel frames, which are much stronger, are more suited to large-scale high-volume use, although their weight and cost make them much less attractive to small-scale users.

When buying a screen you need to consider the inside size of the frame and not just the outside size. The inside size of

Screen frames.

T-shirt printer's workshop.

9

the screen frame will govern the size of the image that can be successfully printed. There should be room for the ink and your squeegee to rest while you are not printing. As a general rule, allow at least 15cm top and bottom and 10cm at the sides if you want to avoid tricky technical problems. It is also useful to stick to some standard sizes, so that you can also standardize the size of your coating troughs, drying cabinet and so on. It is also a good idea to have a set of smaller screens available, rather than to think that one big screen will be more economical because you can put multiple images on to it. Unless you plan very carefully, having multiple images on one big screen will mean lots of masking out and awkward printing positions further down the line. A larger screen will also stretch differently at the centre than at the edges, thus affecting the registration of layers in your print.

Screen meshes

Most meshes used today are made of monofilament polyester. This is single-thread polyester woven into a very smooth regular fabric supplied in many different mesh counts. Polyester mesh will still stretch out of shape and in an industrial setting where accuracy is key, such as the electronics industry, the meshes would be made of stainless-steel wire, or even liquid crystal polymer.

The mesh count refers to the number of strands per centimetre (in the EU) or per inch (in the USA). If you are buying a ready-stretched frame, the mesh count will usually be written with a permanent marker on the glued side of the frame expressed as a figure followed by a letter, for example 77T. A 77T mesh will have exactly 77 strands per centimetre. The T stands for the thread diameter. Polyester thread is produced in three different thicknesses: S (small); T (medium); and HD (heavy duty). The mesh count and the diameter of the thread controls what is known as the mesh geometry. This geometry ultimately controls the amount and type of ink that can pass through the mesh. It also controls both the thickness of the layer of ink that will be deposited and the fineness and crispness of detail that can be printed through it. For industrial purposes, this can be calculated very accurately. Very fine or heavy-duty meshes are usually the reserve of automated machinery and fast or slow moving print presses. Medium (T) meshes are the most suitable for work printed by hand on an ordinary screen bed, so these are what most people working on a hand bench would use.

Online or in suppliers' catalogues there may be other shorthand descriptive letters, such as W or Y. These refer to the colour of the mesh, white and yellow being the most common. Yellow meshes are usually above 90T and are used for exposing detailed photo stencils such as halftones because they absorb more light and prevent it from scattering and undercutting fine lines and details. Other common letters are PW and TW, which refer to plain weave and twill weave. Twill-weave meshes will be slightly thicker and sturdier than plain weave, but will deposit slightly less ink even if the mesh count is the same. The chart shows commonly used European mesh counts and their American equivalents.

Mesh count on screen.

MESH COUNTS

EU mesh count	US mesh count	EU mesh count	US mesh count
34T	86	77T	196
43T	110	90T	230
49T	125	100T	255
55T	140	110T	280
62T	158	120T	305

Mesh counts from 34–62 (EU) are generally used for fabric printing, or for printing with speciality inks that contain, for example, metallics, mica or reflective glass beads. If you have a particular project in mind, a quick look through any trade catalogue from a screen-printing supplier will soon reveal just how many specialist applications there are and it makes sense to refer to the ink manufacturer's technical specifications when deciding which mesh to choose. Most manufacturers have proactive technical departments who will be happy to answer questions about their products, or have FAQs on their website where most answers can be found.

Finer screens from 77T to 120T and beyond are used mostly for paper or board and other less absorbent materials. A good general purpose screen to choose for printing on paper with water-based inks would be a 90T or 120T. For fabric, a 55T or a 49T would be more suitable. Obviously the finer the screen, the more vulnerable it will be to damage, which is why you will rarely find screens above 77T or 90T in most schools or colleges.

Screen meshes are not particularly cheap and the finer they are, the more expensive they get and the easier they are to 'pop'.

Whatever the mesh, the result will be better if it is properly tensioned on the frame – good registration between layers cannot be achieved if using old and baggy screens. Retensionable screens, known as 'dynamic screens', can be bought, but unless you have a high-volume business, it is probably not worth the expense. Although it is also possible to buy the equipment necessary to stretch and recover your own screens, it takes up valuable space and also the glues used are volatile and not particularly user-friendly. It is probably not worth trying to restretch screens yourself unless you are turning over a lot of work and it would prove economical to do so. Overall, unless you are working on a medium to large scale, it is better to buy in ready-stretched 'static' screens and save up the inevitable casualties until you have enough to send a batch away to a specialist restretching company.

Squeegees

A squeegee consists of a polyurethane blade fixed into a wooden or metal handle (usually aluminium). There are also combination squeegees, which have a wooden grip and metal plates to hold the blade in place.

The hardness of the polyurethane is measured in durometers and expressed as a double digit number from 50 to 95A. The lowest number represents the softest blade and the highest the

Squeegees.

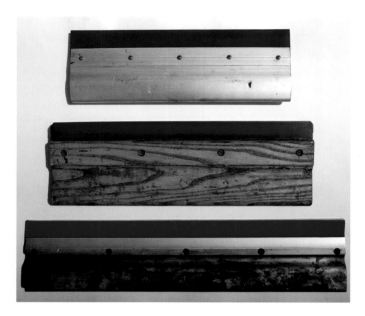

Different types of squeegee.

durometer squeegee blades that combine the virtues of two or three different hardnesses of blade into one. However, for most purposes, when printing on paper the standard green medium blade will be fine.

Secondly, squeegee blades can be bought with different profiles. Rectangular squeegees are suitable for most types of printing, but there are others. A 'V'-shaped squeegee is used to print on rounded surfaces such as bottles or jars, while rounded squeegees will put down a thick layer of ink for fabric printing. The latter, however, will not give the same sharp edge to the print as a rectangular blade, so that printing sharp detail may not be possible.

Lastly, you will need to consider the length of the squeegees that you want to buy. Ideally, you would want to have a number of squeegees of different lengths including some small ones, which often come in very handy.

The squeegee needs to be roughly 2–4cm longer than the width of the image you are printing. The aim is to print in one pull, so the squeegee needs to be wide enough to do this easily. Although it is possible to print with a squeegee that is too long, a successful print cannot be achieved with one that is too short. It also needs to fit inside the frame comfortably. Have it too close to the edge of the frame and you will not be able to make contact with the table underneath because of the snap-off (the gap between the mesh and the tabletop; *see* Chapter 7). At this point the mesh is very tight because it is glued to the frame and it will not stretch far enough to allow contact with the table. If your squeegee is too wide, you will not be able to print the edges of your print properly and, even worse, will risk ripping your expensive mesh.

hardest. Generally, the blade is manufactured in one of three colours, red, green and blue, where red is the softest, green is medium and blue is hard.

Firstly, the softer the squeegee, the more ink is forced through the mesh, so soft squeegees are used for fabric printing or when printing on to rough materials like canvas that need a lot of coverage. Hard squeegees will print less ink and are suitable for printing on to smooth or non-absorbent surfaces, thus they are good for detail. It is also possible to get dual and even triple

Squeegee blade and fixings.

Things to look out for in second-hand squeegees

If the blade is worn or rounded, or is starting to come out of its handle and is not completely flat, you will have trouble printing successfully. You should be able to unscrew the handle and push the blade flat again. If there are nicks in the blade, these will show as dark lines in the print, especially in a translucent colour. So run your finger along it and feel for any inconsistencies. Sometimes the cure is as simple as remembering to turn the squeegee around, then printing and flooding using the undamaged side. Although there are specialized machines for resharpening squeegee blades, at a push it is possible to fix a nicked blade by sticking a length of medium to fine emery paper to a board or bench and carefully rubbing the edge of the blade at right angles backwards and forwards along its length. It is easy to replace blades if necessary.

Sometimes the screws in the handle will also need drilling out and replacing, as they tend to rust or get clogged with ink and the screw heads become damaged over time.

Screen-printing tables

Ideally, for printing on paper, a vacuum table (also called a screen bed or bench) should be used. There are many different varieties in manufacture, but generally speaking a hand bench (or hand-operated flatbed press) is a hollow, flat table that has been drilled with holes in the print area and is attached

to a vacuum pump. The classic hand bench is a Quad Crown, which refers to its size (not its name or make), meaning that it can print up to 30 × 40in. These measurements hark back to the days of imperial paper sizes that are still in use informally, despite their replacement by modern ISO sizes.

The vacuum is there to prevent the paper from sticking to the ink on the back of the screen. When it is turned on and the screen is down in the printing position, air is sucked through the holes to hold the paper in place. As the screen is raised, a simple sliding mechanism underneath the table uncovers an opening that effectively weakens the suction, allowing you to remove your print and replace it with the next sheet of paper.

There is a frame attached to the bed that has a system of sliding bars and clamps within which you can fix your screen

ABOVE RIGHT: **Screen clamp.**

Typical Quad Crown screen vacuum bed.

so that it will not move out of place while printing. There are many different kinds of clamps, but they all perform the same function.

There are also frames that are hinged at the back of the table and carry counterbalance weights that can be adjusted so that the screen stays down while printing, but can be lifted out of the way in order for the print to be retrieved and put on a rack to dry. Some tables have an internal spring mechanism that performs the same function.

On all four corners of the frame there is a screw mechanism that allows you to control the snap-off, the technical name given to the distance between the screen and the tabletop. This is needed when printing on paper and board, but not when printing on fabric. At the back of the table where the frame is carrying the counterbalance weights, this has to be a substantial device. At the front, however, it can be less solid and takes the form of a large screw with a wing nut that can be tightened to fix it in position. In order to achieve accuracy, it is important to lock everything down once it has been adjusted correctly, so that nothing moves as you put all of that energy through the press when printing an edition. These screen mechanisms have long screws so that the screen can be raised away from the bed

in order to accommodate and print on to thick flat objects such as lumps of wood or glass.

More often than not, the screen table will have a precise registration system, with the bed of the press tensioned on springs

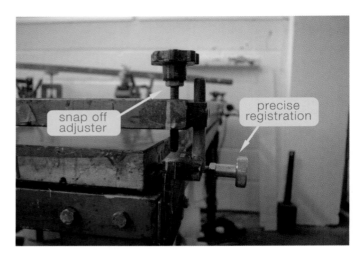

Precise registration and snap-off devices at the front edge of the table.

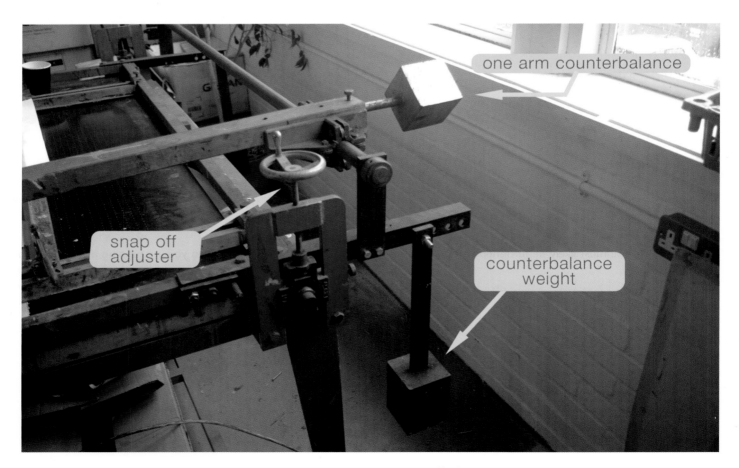

Counterbalance weights and snap-off adjuster.

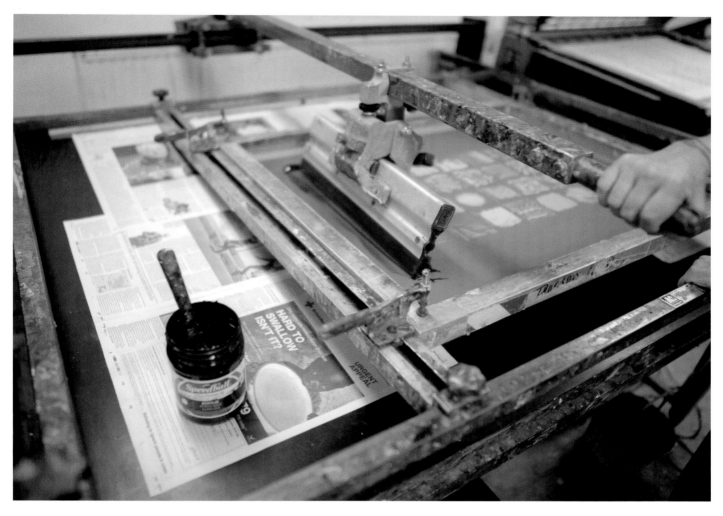

One-arm squeegee holder in action.

positioned underneath. At three points (the magic registration number), it will be possible to move the whole bed by fractional amounts, thus enabling you to tweak the print into position under the screen and sort out tiny misregistrations.

Also, the bed will most likely be furnished with a 'one arm', that is, a holder for the squeegee. This allows you to pull the squeegee from side to side across the bed with the squeegee clamped in the one arm at just the right angle for the flood stroke and the print stroke. The one arm evens out the stroke and if balanced correctly (it has its own counterbalance weight) takes the effort out of printing and makes it significantly easier to print large areas.

Professionals would always use the one arm, even when printing small things, because it makes the process more accurate. You may want the handmade look of bad registration for fashionable reasons, but it would be nice if it were repeatable across the edition, rather than being a random accident due to bad technique.

Handmade benches

Many people want to print at home or in their studio, but do not have the space for a vacuum bed. In workshop situations in schools and colleges, or when you are running a workshop on the move, quite often there is no space or budget for having screen tables as a permanent fixture, in which case a perfectly acceptable cheap and cheerful alternative would be to build your own temporary set-up using hinges or jiffy clamps.

Jiffy clamps are preferable to hinges because they have a built-in snap-off for the back of the frame due to the thickness of the metal and do not require anything to be screwed into the screen frame itself (difficult with an aluminium screen). It is a very simple matter to screw a couple of jiffy clamps into a left-over piece of kitchen worktop or something similar and (wearing a mask) to spray the print area very lightly with pressure-sensitive glue to act like the vacuum. Stick a couple of pieces of card under the front edges of your screen frame (to

Temporary workshop set-up at West Dean College.

Jiffy clamps.

give the snap-off at the front), find something with which to prop it up (like a block of wood) and you are practically ready to print.

The first step-by-step detailed instructions in this book are for a two-colour print using paper stencils printed on a DIY table-top screen bed made using jiffy clamps.

Coating troughs

Coating troughs are also known as scoop coaters. They are lengths of semicircular or 'V'-shaped aluminium with removable end pieces and smooth edges used for holding and applying a thin coating of liquid photographic emulsion to the screen. It is not easy to perform this simple task successfully without

Coating troughs.

one, although many have tried. If you have a number of different-sized screens, you will need several different lengths of trough to accommodate them. Basically, the trough needs to fit within the inside frame size either lengthways or widthways by 3–4cm.

Exposure units

Exposure units are also known as a print-down frames.

Gung-ho methods

Many years ago, as a rookie teenage would-be screenprinter, my art teacher (with, please note, complete disregard for health and safety) showed me how to expose a screen using a packing case with a sun lamp in the bottom, its open top covered with a sheet of plate glass. We would place our positives on the glass and a coated screen on top of that, followed by a piece of foam and a board cut to fit the inside dimensions of the screen. We then piled books on top of the board, covered the whole thing with a bit of black cloth and made a timed exposure.

The point of all that was to hold the positive in tight contact with the emulsion on the screen so that the ultraviolet light from the sunlamp would not creep around the image and undercut it. It worked beautifully, although the exposure time was very long. The magic of making a photostencil for the first time in this way has never left me. For this reason, I would not wish to discourage anyone from having a go at exposing screens without a conventional exposure unit, although it only really works with fail-safe positives that are completely lightproof in the image area.

It is quite possible, for example, to expose a screen simply by taping the positive to the underside of your coated, dried screen with clear tape and holding a sheet of glass over it, backing it with a bit of plywood and tensioning the whole thing with your hands to get the required tight contact. All you have to do then is hold it up to the sunshine (while avoiding looking directly at the sun). It is simple, but also hit and miss, as you can never guarantee the exposure time, plus you have to coat and dry the screen in the dark somewhere first. Bright sunshine will expose a screen almost instantly.

A vacuum bag is the next stop. Sometimes these are used commercially when the screens to be exposed are too large for any normal exposure unit to cope with. You can improvise with a shop-bought vacuum sack meant to store clothes or duvets. Put the coated screen with the positive taped to the underside (the flat side of the screen) inside the bag and suck all the air out with a vacuum cleaner. Note: you will also need to put a sheet of card on the inside of the frame to protect this side from the light. You can either then expose this to the sunshine, or use a free-hanging ultraviolet bulb. Again, the exposure times will be a matter of trial and error and, if using the bulb, will depend on its wattage and the distance between it and the screen. The only way to be more precise is to use a commercial unit. These come in many guises.

A print-down frame consists of a sheet of plate glass hinged to a frame in-filled with a neoprene rubber sheet. The whole frame is supported on a stand that allows it to be swung from a horizontal position, so that you can put your positive and screen in place, into an upright position, so that the screen inside can face the light. The whole contraption is attached to a vacuum pump. When the frame is clamped shut, all of the air between the glass and the rubber sheet can be pumped out. This ensures that the screen and positive do not slip out of place when the unit is in the upright position and also that there is the necessary very tight contact between emulsion and positive for the exposure to be successful.

This kind of frame assumes access to a free-standing exposure lamp that can be adjusted to the right height and distance to make the required exposure. The diagonal of the largest screen should be measured and the lamp placed at least this distance away from the unit when making the exposure. This type of unit, where a single light source is at a distance from the target, will give the best possible conditions for exposing fine lines and details like halftones without undercutting the positive. However, since there is nothing to stop the operator from being exposed to the very bright ultraviolet light, this type of exposure has to be done in a separate room or in an enclosed space. Looking at the light directly would be very bad for the operator's eyes.

Self-contained exposure units

In a busy environment where there are going to be many people around, a self-contained unit is safer than the above methods. A unit like this is basically a lightproof box containing the light source. This can be either a mercury vapour lamp, or a series of fluorescent tubes or bulbs. This is topped with a sheet of plate glass and a hinged rubber lid. The positive and screen are placed between the glass and the rubber in the same way as described above and the air is pumped out to create a vacuum.

This style of unit does not need to be in a separate room. The unit pictured is a variation on the theme, since it incorporates a drying cabinet underneath to save space. In this particular case the light is suspended above the glass. There is a slight disadvantage in enclosed units, in that the light source is always at a fixed distance from the target. Very large screens may be exposed unevenly, since the single-spot light source burns more brightly in the middle and falls away towards the edges of the box. To avoid undercutting, it is best if the light falls at direct right angles to the target rather than coming in from the side, thus it may not be possible to expose fine lines and halftones quite so well. This is even more true of exposure units with strip lights or bulbs, where the light comes from many different directions and is even closer to the target.

ABOVE: **Picture of self-contained unit, including drying cabinet.**

Small unit with fluorescent tubes.

Drying cabinets

Whether it is necessary to have one of these for drying coated and washed-out screens depends upon the volume of work that passes through the workshop. Coated screens are light-sensitive and therefore have to be dried in the dark, or in safety lighting (red or yellow). An individual might make do with a dark cupboard and a fan heater on the cool setting for drying screens, although to get the best result screens should be dried flat, preferably flat side down. This may seem counter-intuitive, but having a thicker coating on the flat side of the screen (the side that goes down on to the paper) gives a sharper, cleaner edge to the stencil and therefore a better print. Drying the screen with the flat side down allows most of the emulsion to sink through to the back of the screen (the flat side). Drying the screen upright will allow the emulsion to slide towards the ground. The resulting stencil will be thinner at the top than the bottom, making the exposure uneven. These differences are very small and probably would not bother most hobby or artist printers, but they can make a big difference when exposing detail.

It is worth noting that this is one of the reasons why indirect capillary stencils are sometimes better at printing detail than direct stencils, which are liquid emulsions coated directly on to the screen. An indirect stencil is an acetate-backed layer of emulsion usually bought on a roll. This 'film' is exposed to a positive in the same way as a direct stencil. It is applied to a dampened screen after the exposure and development have taken place, hence the name 'indirect'. Capillary action 'sucks' the soft stencil emulsion into the mesh, forming a very even layer. These sorts of stencils are often used for high-end screen-printing on fine meshes to produce ultra-fine halftones and lines.

A commercial drying cabinet will have mesh-bottomed drawers or movable metal supports to accommodate the screens, which slide in and dry flat. Other advantages of commercial drying cabinets are that they are temperature-controlled and have fans to keep the air circulating evenly, so that the screens inside are not subject to hot spots, which can 'expose' the emulsion. Because they are enclosed and have air filters, they also have fewer dust problems.

They do, however, take up a lot of space. I know at least one printer who dries his screens under a large table that has been surrounded with heavy black polythene, so that the space taken up is at least dual-purpose. Another solution is to have an 'all in one' drying cabinet and exposure unit, like the one at Inkspot Press pictured here.

Washouts

Once the screen has been exposed, it needs washing to clear away the unexposed, unhardened emulsion, so you need access to a water supply with a hose attachment and some kind of water trough big enough to accommodate your largest screens.

Some people make do with a garden hose with spray attachments. This is fine for washing out stencils, but for cleaning and recycling screens where ink may have dried in, or stencils have hardened, a pressure washer is invaluable. This does not need to be an industrial version – one from your local DIY store will do just fine. Cleaning screens can be a messy business. If using a pressure wash, there will be a lot of noise as well. So cleaning

Washout trough at the University of Brighton.
Note the use of yellow lighting to avoid accidental
exposure of unexposed screens.

Screen cleaning with a pressure wash (Jamie Stephen-Mitchel, at the University of Brighton).

screens is best done in a separate room away from other activities and ear protection should always be worn.

You can make do with one unit for washing off ink, washing out stencils and recycling screens, but, ideally, if you have the space, a separate backlit booth that stays clean (one with a frosted Perspex insert in the back with strip lights behind) is great for checking that you have washed out your stencils correctly.

Racks

The ideal way to dry screenprints is on a purpose-made rack, which allows air to circulate all around the print. These come in several different sizes, but usually have fifty trays, which are sprung-loaded so that they stay up in the air out of the way until the next print is ready. They are also on wheels so that they can be moved around the studio. You can also buy small tabletop varieties, although the trays are not always sprung – the prints just slot into place.

Prints drying on a purpose-made rack.

Picture of small tabletop rack.

The simplest rack is a ball rack. This consists of a plank of wood with shapes cut out at regular intervals that will hold a glass marble. The marble is kept in place by a simple piece of bent wire on either side. This contraption is hung from the ceiling.

A ball rack.

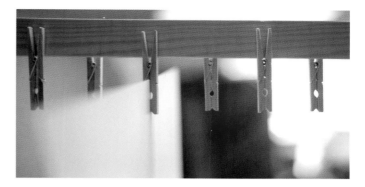

Pegs glued along a baton of wood.

The print is pushed up against the marble and the weight of the marble keeps it in place so that it hangs vertically.

You can make a simple DIY version of this using pegs glued at regular intervals along a baton of wood. In fact, the peg hanging system can have many cheap and ingenious permutations; washing line with cut straws as spacers for the pegs, for example, or skirt hangers lined up along a rail.

A double washing line using pegs with straws as spacers.

Photoemulsions

Direct emulsions

Screen emulsions consist of a polyvinyl alcohol or polyvinyl acetate base that is sensitized with either a diazo photo-sensitizer or an SBQ (Styrl Basolium Quaternary) photopolymer. Emulsions react to ultraviolet (UV) light. Exposure to the light makes them harden, or 'cure'. Even daylight has enough UV to harden screen emulsions, although it would take time. This is why it is preferable to handle emulsions in yellow or red safe-light conditions, or at the very least in subdued light. They also react to excessive heat, which is why exposing a coated and dried screen in the sunlight can be problematic.

Diazo emulsions are slower and have a wide exposure latitude, but are not quite as good at reproducing fine detail as the SBQ photopolymers, which are faster, have a small exposure latitude but are more expensive. Exposure latitude means the extent to which a light-sensitive material can be overexposed or underexposed and still give a good result.

There are dual-cure emulsions that combine the best qualities of both of the above, having a mid-range exposure time that can reproduce fine detail well and are not as expensive as SBQ emulsions. If using water-based inks, you need to check that the emulsion you have chosen is water-resistant, as some are only resistant to solvent-based inks. Dual-cure emulsions can often be formulated to resist both water and solvent, which is useful if you do not want to stock both types.

Diazo and dual-cure emulsions come in two parts – the base emulsion and a sensitizer (SBQ emulsion is mixed by the manufacturer, so comes ready to use.) The sensitizer is provided in a dark-coloured bottle and consists of a powder that needs to be dissolved by filling the sensitizer bottle with warm water and shaking it up. Take care when handling the sensitizer, as it has a powerful yellow stain – if you don't want to look like a heavy smoker, wear gloves. Pour the sensitizer into the pot of emulsion and mix thoroughly (preferably with a wooden stirrer rather than a metal one) and allow it to stand, so that any bubbles formed can disperse before using. Remember that it is light-sensitive so must be kept covered. Once they have been mixed, the emulsions have a shelf life that can be prolonged by keeping them in a fridge.

Screen filler (or screen block)

Screen filler is often used to spot out pinholes in the hardened photostencil, which have been caused by dust on the glass of the exposure unit. Some makes are waterproof when dry, while others resist only solvent-based inks, so be careful which you buy. There are also kinds that resist both water and solvent. The water-resistant variety can be removed from the screen with stencil remover. You can, of course, use screen filler to paint whole stencils, a negative method of working (*see* Chapter 4). In combination with screen drawing fluid, it can also be adapted to produce a positive working stencil (*see* Chapter 5).

Haze remover

Over time, a screen can build up stains and ink deposits. If they can still be seen through when holding the screen up to the light, they will cause few problems. However, they will eventually 'ghost back' and begin to show up in new prints. Haze remover products, which are caustic, remove these residues, but they are often hazardous. Care must be taken to wear the right protective clothing and a mask. Less hazardous and bio-degradable is the old-fashioned 'Pink Stuff', which has been around since the 1930s and can still be bought commercially. It is an abrasive paste made of silica and vegetable soap. It is slightly alkaline and works surprisingly well to remove both acrylic- and oil-based ink deposits if scrubbed into the mesh with a soft brush.

Digital printers

For printing out digital positives you will need access to a printer, either laser or inkjet. It is perfectly possible to produce good-quality positives on an ordinary A4 inkjet printer using OHP film (overhead-projection film), which is widely available in most stationers. The A4 size will be the biggest restriction. An A3 inkjet printer is useful, but A3 inkjet film can often only be sourced online and in boxes of 100 sheets, so the expense makes it a real commitment. Inkjet printers can be notoriously expensive to run. A4 or A3 mono laser printers are a lot more economical (it is not necessary to have a colour printer to print positives). Since these are thermal printers, you need the correct heat-resistant film to run through them. They often come with a built-in PostScript RIP (Raster Image Processor), which is useful for printing proper halftones, so look carefully at the specifications if you are selecting one.

If you want to go bigger, then you either send your files away to an online bureau to be printed, or invest in a large-format printer. Try finding out about your nearest open-access print-making studio. They often offer positive-making services if they have a large-format printer. Some of the bigger and more well-established ones will also offer an online service.

Obviously if you are running a small business, it would make sense to have your own large-format printer once you are established. These days, it is possible to hire them. This often has the added advantage of a repair contract and the opportunity to buy, for a nominal amount, at the end of the lease, or to have an upgrade to a newer model. However, if you are planning to print a lot of halftones, you will have to buy a separate bit of software (a dedicated RIP) for inkjet printers to get them to perform this function. Many of these programs can be maddeningly full of unnecessary bells and whistles and very expensive. Much research is needed before you take this particular plunge. There are many colour separation packages on the market, most of which are aimed at the T-shirt printer.

Often it is possible to try before you buy on a limited time span. This is probably a good idea, because you can search out any software incompatibility problems before you commit. You may well also find some freeware on the Internet if you search around.

Inks

This book is primarily aimed at people who are using water-based inks. This is the system now preferred for use in schools and colleges and by individual artists and designers in their own studios, where easy clean-up and health and safety issues are paramount. It is a commonly held misconception that acrylic-based inks are more environmentally friendly. This may be true of the immediate environment of the printer, that is, in your studio, but they are still a product of the petrochemical industry and may still contain some toxic colours and chemicals. To find out what they do contain, it is a good idea to refer

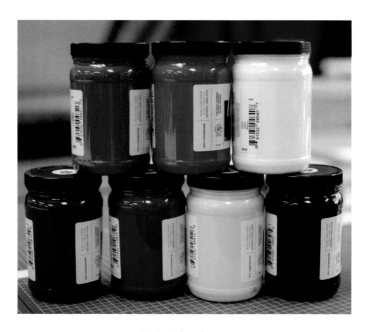

Basic ink colours.

to the particular manufacturer's product safety sheets, which are easily accessible online. What is great about acrylic inks is that they can be cleaned up with water rather than the volatile solvents used when cleaning up oil-based inks. From this point of view, they are much safer to use in a small workshop or studio that does not have a dedicated extraction and ventilation system.

Although there are still some effects that can only be successfully produced using oil-based inks (high gloss, for example), for ease of use, low odour and low VOCs (volatile organic compounds), water-based inks have distinct advantages for the artist. They are capable of printing on most substrates, such as paper, textiles, metal, plastics and wood, and their accessibility has made it easier for individuals to experiment with the medium. There are currently three kinds of water-based ink systems available to the artist.

Ready-mixed acrylic silkscreenprinting inks

These are usually subdivided into inks suitable for paper and those with additives that allow them to be heat-cured and are for use on fabrics. Major manufacturers of these inks are Speedball, Permaset, Jacquard and Cadisch, amongst others. These inks can be used straight from the pot, colour-mixed with each other, or mixed with a transparent base to make them more translucent for overprinting. In addition to the usual painters' colour range, there is an exciting range of different options, such as opaque, metallic, pearlescent, iridescent, fluorescent, interference colours and glow in the dark.

Pigment systems

Some manufacturers, such as TW Graphics and Dave Roper for example, supply a different system based on concentrated pigments that are added to either transparent or opaque bases, to allow you to fine-tune the printed effects. The latter inks are more akin to the 'tinters' used in oil-based systems to bump up the colour. They tend to dry in the mesh a lot faster (although retardants are available to counteract this) and, because of the intensity of the colour, will stain the meshes if not cleaned up quickly enough. In use they behave more like an oil-based ink, so beginners may prefer to start with something a little more forgiving until they are up to speed.

Acrylic paint

Most of the artists' acrylic paint manufacturers, such as Winsor and Newton, Daler-Rowney, Lascaux, Golden, Spectrum

and others, supply acrylic screen-printing media, which, when mixed with their paints, will make them printable. There are two types, one for paper, board and so on, and one for fabric, which is fixable with heat.

The screen-printing media have three functions when mixed with acrylic paint. They give it a more flowing texture with which to print. They act as transparent media to reduce opacity in the colours for overprinting and brilliance. But, most importantly, they contain retardants to slow the drying time of the acrylic paint. If printed on its own, acrylic paint will dry really quickly in the screen and also in a thin film on top of the stencil. Once dry, it is very difficult to clean off – your stencils would very quickly become blocked and you would lose all the detail in your print. The dried film of ink on top of the stencil also makes reclaiming the screen much more difficult, since it prevents the stencil remover from making contact with the stencil. Ink dried in the mesh usually needs more than just water and a pressure gun to clean it out.

Obviously the colour ranges of these paints are based on an artist's palette, although most manufacturers have also added a set of process colours – cyan, magenta, process yellow and process black (CMYK) – to their lists. Like the CMYK setting on your computer, they are designed for four-colour process printing and will give true, more predictable, overprints. They are some of the most useful colours that a screenprinter can own, because from these four colours you can, at least in theory, make all the colours of the rainbow. With the addition of cadmium red, ultramarine blue, black and white, they are a good minimum set of colours to start up with.

Mixing the inks is a simple matter of adding medium to acrylic. The more medium, the more translucent the colour and the more overprints it will be possible to produce (where one translucent colour prints over another to create a third). A minimum of 20 per cent medium to acrylic is generally the most opaque mix that will still be retarded from drying in the screen. If you are a beginner or a bit rusty and are liable to be slow at first, a mix of 50 × 50 per cent is a good place to start. The inks should have a 'dropping' consistency like double cream or thin pancake batter. If you pick up a spoonful, it should slide and drop off the spoon. If it is too thick to do this, let it down with a drop of cold water. Leftover inks will keep for a long time if covered. If they have thickened up, they can be revived with a drop of water and some extra screen medium.

Papers

The type and colour of the paper used can change both the behaviour of the ink and the overall colour and look of the print. So it is very important that you choose the right type for the work in hand – something that is going to enhance your work but also be cost-effective, which is a delicate balance to achieve. Traditionally, most printmakers prefer to work on handmade or mould-made papers (papers made on a cylinder mould dipped and rotated in a vat of paper pulp). Also, they prefer to use a paper made with cotton rag rather than those made from wood pulp. The reason for this is simply one of longevity. It would be a shame to put so much work into a print and then have it yellow with age, or break out in spots (called foxing) due to contaminants in the paper-making process. However, there are also good machine-made papers available that will be more than suitable. It really depends on what market you are trying to reach with your prints and price you are hoping to sell them for.

Handmade paper has a deckled edge with a ragged look that is named after the wooden frame, or 'fence', used to frame each sheet. This allows some of the paper pulp to creep under the frame, giving a rough edge. It is a bit of a status symbol, although not widely understood outside of the watercolour, bookbinding or printmaking fraternity. Mould-made paper usually has only two deckled edges, the other two being torn (to look deckled), or cut straight. When screen-printing, the deckle often has to be cut off, at least where the registration stops are going to be, since a straight edge is needed for this purpose.

Whether the paper is handmade or machine-made, made of rag or wood pulp, most artists or designers would want to work on paper that is 'acid free' (sometimes called neutral pH). These are papers made with neutral sizing, which will not deteriorate as quickly as others. Sizing gives the paper its water resistance. A paper might be sized with gelatin, Aquapel or rosin, for example, and can be hard-sized, soft-sized or unsized. Hard-sized paper that is suitable for watercolour would be good for screen-printing if using a water-based ink. A soft-sized paper might absorb more of the ink, thus softening and changing its colour and appearance on the paper. This may be a highly desirable and beautiful effect, but it might also cockle (buckle) as it dries, thus creating problems when registering colour layers.

Water-based screenprinters need to work on papers that are heavy in weight to avoid the cockling problem as much as possible. Since metrification, the weight of paper is expressed in grams per square metre, abbreviated to gsm or g/m^2. The higher the figure of gsm, the heavier the paper. As a general rule, only papers that are over 200gsm are suited to water-based screenprinting and if large, flat areas of colour are involved, it would be advisable to use even heavier papers at between 300 and 400gsm.

The surface of the paper has to be considered too. It would be pointless, for example, to try to print a halftone or fine lines on a rough-surfaced paper. The most common paper surfaces are expressed as HP, NOT and Rough. HP stands for 'hot pressed', where the paper has been ironed, so to speak, between hot metal plates to give it a smooth surface. NOT stands for 'not hot pressed', which gives a matt, semi-rough surface. Rough stands for paper that has been pressed up against rough felts as a part of its manufacture and therefore has a textured surface.

Halftones and fine lines would print better on a hot-pressed, non-absorbent surface, for example. Most screenprinters spend a lot of time researching the right paper for the job in hand and will, over time, amass a list of favourites for their particular colour or surface quality. The specialist suppliers of printmaking papers will happily give advice on the suitability of their papers if you contact them with information about what the paper is going to be used for.

Staying safe

If setting up a communal workshop or simply to look after yourself, it is essential to refer to current Government health and safety guidelines. In the UK, this means looking at the COSHH (Control of Substances Hazardous to Health) that are essential for printers. These are published by the Government HSE (Health and Safety Executive) and are available online. Page 24 (on 'Manual Screen Reclamation') is a very useful starting point (http://www.hse.gov.uk/pubns/guidance/p24.pdf), since the most hazardous part of the screen-printing process is the cleaning and recycling of screens. Wearing protective gear will save both you and your clothing from unnecessary exposure to any chemicals.

Respirators

When cleaning screens and removing stencils, it is always a good idea to protect your lungs from airborne spray by wearing a half-mask respirator fitted with combined organic vapour/particulate filters that have an APF (assigned protection factor) of ten or more. You will find these in almost any builders' merchants or machine supply shop and in most DIY outlets.

Gloves

It is advisable to wear protective gloves, especially when cleaning screens and handling paints and emulsions. Not all gloves are the same. Ordinary rubber gloves for washing up or surgical gloves do not offer enough protection. They are not impervious to all chemicals and paradoxically, because of this, can allow your skin to be in contact with the bad stuff for longer than wearing no gloves at all. The safest option is to go for chemical-resistant industrial nitrile gloves at least 0.4mm thick. Long gauntlets will protect from splashes when reclaiming screens.

It is also a good idea to use a barrier cream on your hands before starting work, as this will make it much easier to clean up your inky fingers and fingernails later on. A good citrus-based hand cleaner with some pumice content is perfect for cleaning the ink from your hands. You should never clean them with solvent or spirit.

Goggles

Simple plastic goggles will protect your eyes from splashes when blasting screens, but you should have access to an eye-wash facility just in case.

Ear protection

Pressure washing in a confined space is very loud, so ear protectors should always be worn.

Apron

When printing, an ordinary apron will do, but when cleaning screens an impervious waterproof apron is better.

Kitted out for cleaning screens.

CHAPTER 3

USING PAPER STENCILS

Paper stencils are a great way to start learning about the process of screenprinting. They are one of the simplest ways of creating an image, and are cheap and relatively easy to make. Not much equipment is needed, so they can be done at home. The disadvantage is that they do not last long and if you make mistakes, or want to clean down and change colour, the stencil probably will not survive the process. Since you are cutting the stencils by hand, the designs can be as simple or as complicated as you want to make them.

Many prints make use of paper stencil work at some stage in their development. It is often the case that a paper stencil is the easiest way to block off part of an image so that it can be printed in another colour later on, using the same stencil. This can speed up the progress of a print enormously and also allows for last-minute changes.

In this example, we are using a homemade tabletop print bed made out of a piece of leftover kitchen worktop and a pair of jiffy clamps. We are drying the prints by hanging them up on a simple homemade clothes-peg system. The image is by illustrator Anthony Downey and is in two colours, black and grey, although it also uses the white of the paper to emphasize the whites of his character's eyes and the light at the top of the well.

You should use a thin, lightweight paper for the stencil. If the paper is too thick, the squeegee will not be able to force the ink through sharp corners or small holes. It will also cause a build-up of ink next to the cut edges of the paper. Your print will have thick, darker-looking edges and small details, or narrow lines will not print successfully. Also, a thicker stencil material may not stick to the back of the screen properly.

Materials and equipment

- chosen image
- newsprint – it is thin and absorbent, so it sticks well to the back of the screen
- or freezer paper – it has a thin plastic backing on one side, which makes it durable
- or tissue paper – it is so thin that it lets a little ink through, creating subtle textures rather than a flat colour.
- lightbox or window for tracing
- masking tape or magic tape
- scalpel or craft knife
- swivel knife – great if you want to cut intricate curves
- cutting mat
- screen filler
- old loyalty card (or similar) to use as a scraper
- hairdryer
- parcel tape, preferably vinyl tape, as this won't leave its glue behind on the screen
- soft pencil
- jiffy clamps
- spray mount or other pressure-sensitive glue
- face mask (for when using spray glue)
- paper
- inks for printing
- squeegee
- wooden block (or similar) for propping up the screen
- bucket of cold water and a sponge for cleaning up
- large sheet of acetate (bigger than the paper on which you intend to print) or similar translucent water-resistant material (not tracing paper or greaseproof paper, which will cockle when wet).

The size of the screen frame will govern the size of the image that can be printed. You cannot print right up to the edges of a screen frame when printing on paper. There should be some space for the ink and your squeegee to rest while you are not using them. As a general rule, allow at least 15cm top and bottom and 10cm at the sides. Also check the size of your squeegee – it needs to be at least 2cm longer than the width of the image you are printing and must also fit inside the frame comfortably.

Method

1. Draw up the image at the scale you want to use it. You could use a photocopy or a digital printout to help you do this.

2. Tape the image to a lightbox or window, then tape your stencil material over the top of it. Use magic tape or masking tape to cause less damage. Trace the image on to it. We are using newsprint as the stencil material.

3. On a cutting mat, carefully cut out those parts of the image that you want to print in a particular colour. In this instance, Anthony is cutting out the grey areas. Remember that where you want to print needs to be cut out, leaving a hole.

4. When you have finished your cutting, prepare the screen for printing by masking out a border. Place the clean screen on top of the paper stencil. Position it so that there is plenty of room all around it. You could simply mask out the edges of the screen with vinyl tape. This would be faster, but is much less reliable. A more permanent border can be used over and over again.

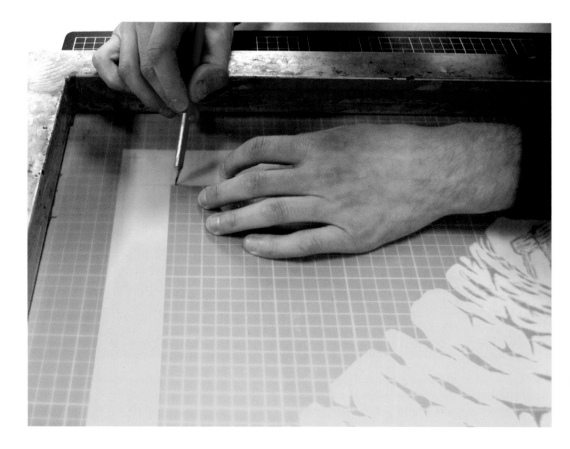

5. Using a soft pencil, make a mark on the mesh at all four corners of the image so that you know where to mask.

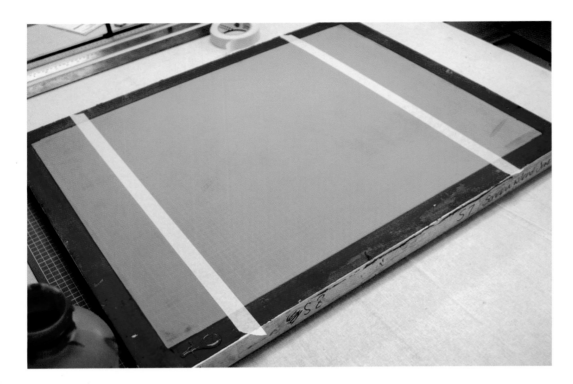

6. To mask out the screen with screen filler, use the marked corners as guides. Stick two lines of masking tape across the screen corresponding to the top and bottom of your image. The lines of tape should be on the inside of your image area.

7. Pour a small bead of screen filler on to the edge of the frame and then, using a scraper, drag the filler across the screen. Keep the scraper at right angles to the screen mesh while doing this, or you will push too much filler through to the other side, resulting in a very thick and uneven layer. The idea is to keep it as thin and even as possible. You should cross over on to the tape, but not so far that filler is accidentally pushed into the printing area.

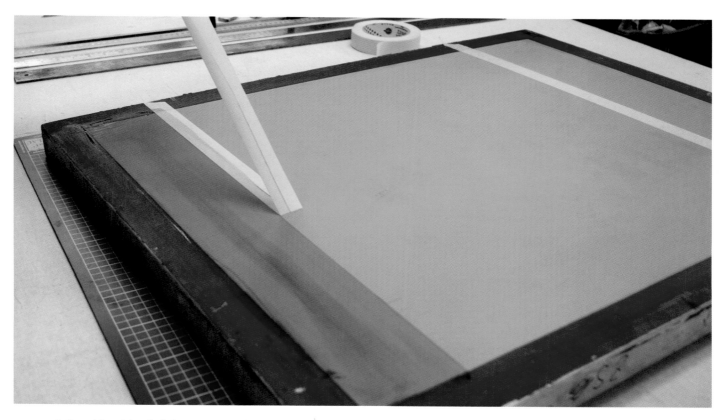

8. Dry this with a hairdryer on a cool setting. Keep the hairdryer moving, if you heat up the polyester mesh too much it will melt. Peel off the tape to leave a nice straight edge.

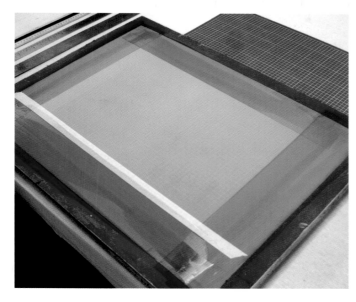

9. Note that it is easiest to do the top and bottom first, then dry them, followed by both sides (or *vice versa*), because in this way you can create regular corners.

10. Tape up on the inside of the screen using vinyl tape. The tape should be positioned so that it bridges the gap between the screen filler and the inside edge of the frame, but also goes up the side of the frame. This stops ink from leaking through the sides of the screen and it will be much easier to clean up at the end. It also keeps your frames in good condition.

11. You are now ready to print the first colour. Clamp the screen into the jiffy clamps.

12. The jiffy clamps will give enough snap-off at the back of the screen frame but not at the front, so attach some thick card to the underside of each front corner to give the necessary lift.

13. Using masking tape, attach the original drawing to one of your pieces of printing paper in the correct position. Turn the paper over and attach a couple of thin card 'handles' to the bottom edge of your paper with masking tape.

14. Position the paper under the screen. The handles cleverly allow you to move the paper around under the screen until it is in the correct place without having to lift the screen up and down.

15. Prepare three register stops. These should be made of very thin card or plastic stuck down with masking tape or double-sided tape. Make sure that the tape butts right up to the edge of the stop, otherwise it is all too easy for the paper to slide under it and the registration will never be accurate. The thin card or plastic allows you to 'bump' the paper into position against the stops each time you position a new sheet and is much better than using tape on its own.

16. Position the three stops on one corner and one edge of the paper. These mark where the paper has to be put down each time. You will register by the same corner and edge for every colour you print from now on. Every print will therefore be in the same relationship to these three points, enabling you to match up the layers successfully. The professionals call this the lay edge.

17. Using acetate or vinyl mark resist for positioning. The first layer of this print is black, but some areas are to be left white (the white of the paper), so the relevant pieces of paper stencil need to go on to the screen in just the right place. To do this without printing on to the master image, take a piece of acetate (or similar) that is big enough to cover the whole print and tape this to the edge of the table on a long hinge of masking tape.

18. It is a good idea to anchor the acetate on the inside as well, so that when it hangs down out of the way, it will not pull itself off.

19. With the acetate 'flopped over' the master image, place the paper stencil pieces in the right position on top of the acetate.

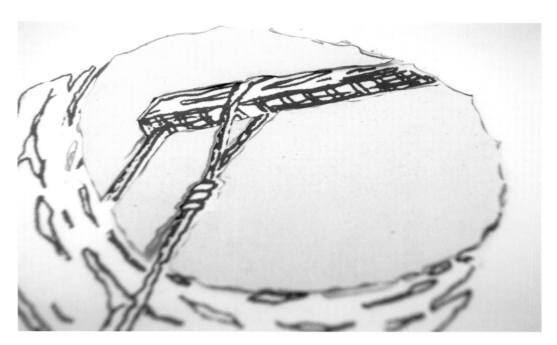

20. Flood the screen with ink. Holding the screen up with one hand, pour a long line of ink (more than you will actually need) along the bottom edge of the image. Place the squeegee behind the roll of ink and hold it at a 45-degree angle, using gentle pressure, push the ink up to the top of the screen to create a thin, even film of ink in the mesh. It is the ink in the mesh that hits the paper, so if the flood stroke is bad or uneven then so is the subsequent print. I like to push the ink with the squeegee angled towards me when flooding, because this gives more control over the 'critical' angle of the blade and a much better reach to the top of the stencil.

21. Print on to the acetate and over the paper stencil pieces. The paper stencil will be picked up by the ink in the screen in the correct position and will stick to the back of the screen. Again, the angle of the squeegee blade is critical. Too low and the ink will 'squelch' through, creating blotchy edges. Too high and too much of the blade will be in contact with the print, which will then most likely laminate itself to the back of the screen. You will know when you have used the correct angle to print because only the sharp edge of the squeegee blade will be in contact with the paper underneath and you will see the screen snapping-off the paper in a neat curve that follows the pull the way down.

22. Flop the acetate out of the way, leaving it hanging down in front of the table. You will only need it again in an emergency registration situation. Remove the master drawing.

23. Place the printing paper in the register stops.

24. Print the first colour on to all the sheets of paper.

25. Hang the prints up to dry. We were using a simple wooden baton with pegs glued to it at regular intervals.

26. When you have finished printing, immediately scrape up all of the leftover ink from the screen and the squeegee. An old store loyalty card or similar is perfect for this. The ink can be kept in a covered pot and used again in the future. If it thickens up, it can be let down again with more screen medium and a drop of water.

27. Peel the stencil off from the back of the screen. If it has stuck, try dampening the top surface of the screen with a sponge.

28. Wash down the acetate with cold water ready to use again for the next colour.

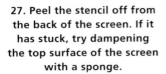

29. Put some newspaper down under the screen and clean as much ink from the top surface as possible using cold water and a sponge or rag. Do not remove the screen from the clamps to clean it. Everything is in register, so if you move the screen you will have to re-register it all again.

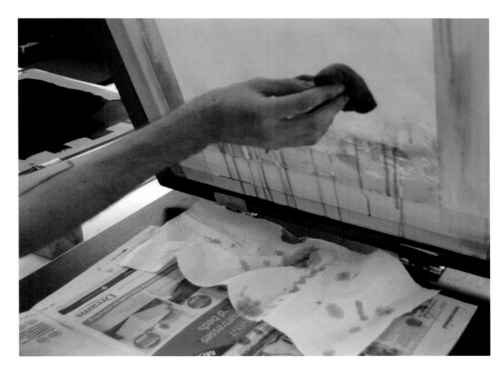

30. Clean the back of the screen with fresh water. For a hefty colour like black, it may take several changes of water to get the screen truly clean again.

31. Set up the second stencil. When the screen and also the first layer of colour are thoroughly dry, use the same procedure to set up the second stencil for the second colour. Replace the master drawing in the register stops and position the paper stencil in the correct position on top of the acetate flop over. Retrieve your prints and stack them the right way up near the print table.

32. Squeegee over the second stencil to pick it up on to the back of the screen.

33. The second stencil on the back of the screen.

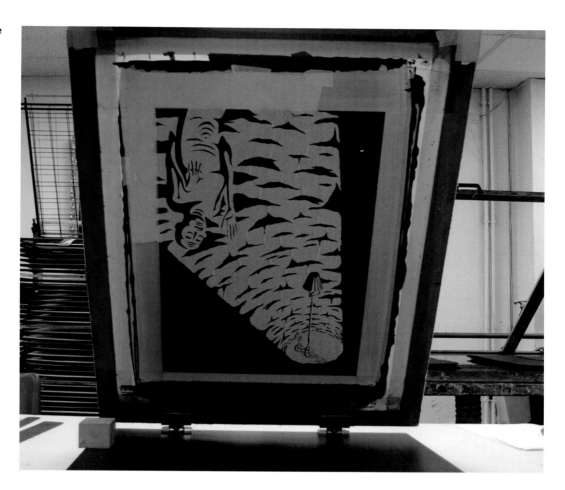

34. Print the second layer. This layer may take longer to dry than the first because the paper is now sealed with a layer of ink and the print can only dry by evaporation, rather than sink into the paper. Continue as before until all of the prints are done. Then scrape up and wash down as before.

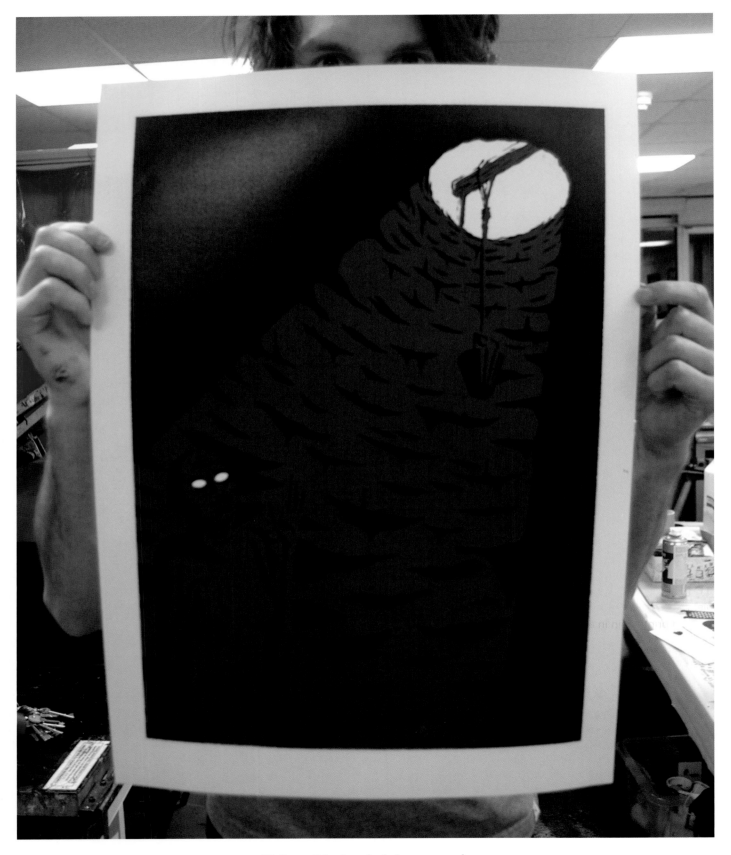

35. Now sit back and admire your work.

CHAPTER 4

REDUCTION PRINTING

Reduction printing is a logical process, whereby the area of stencil that you can print through is reduced, hence the name. The colour layers that make up the print are all painted out on the same screen using screen filler (screen block). If possible, you would want the screen, once in register, to stay set up on the screen table throughout the process. The layers all print directly on top of each other. There are no overprints, in which one colour crosses over another and creates a third. The colours simply mask one another out, although transparent colours may be affected by the colours printed underneath.

You are, in fact, working in negative, painting out what you do not want to print layer by layer. Usually, you start with the lightest colour and work up to the darkest, although this is not a fixed rule, since screen ink can often be mixed opaquely enough to cover the colour underneath. Pastel colours, mixed with a significant amount of white pigment, will, for instance, cover a darker colour.

With this method, there is no going back. Once you have painted something out and the filler has dried on the screen, that area cannot be unblocked unless the painted stencil is cleaned off with stencil remover. It can be combined with any of the other methods described in this book. You may, for example, make up a photostencil and print it, then paint parts of it out and print again in another colour.

Materials and equipment

- master drawing, printout or photocopy, the size that you want your finished print to be
- open screen masked off to the same size as the master image and taped up as in Chapter 3
- soft pencil
- selection of brushes, round and flat
- card or scraper
- screen filler
- squeegee
- inks for printing
- paper
- stencil remover
- pad or soft brush to apply the stencil remover
- pressure wash or garden hose with a jet spray attachment for removing the stencil.

Holding up the drawing.

Method

In the following example, illustrator John Parkinson used a photograph (taken in a museum) as his starting point.

1. Make a scaled-up drawing from the original. It makes life easier if the paper used is the same size as the printing paper.

2. Set up the screen on the print table and line up the drawing under the screen. Mark the registration with three stops as described in Chapter 3.

ABOVE: **3. Using a soft pencil, trace directly on to the screen any areas that you want to remain white (or the colour of the paper) throughout the print. Paint them out with screen filler. When painting, take care to have the screen slightly raised, or the filler will stick to your master drawing.**

4. Print the first colour, in this case the background, then leave it on the rack to dry while you clean up and prepare the screen for the next layer.

5. Clean and dry the screen without taking it off the table (*see* Chapter 3). Put the original drawing underneath once more. Trace and then paint out everything that you want to leave the first colour, in this case the background. You can use a brush for the fiddly outlines and a scraper for large areas.

6. Thoroughly dry the filler using a hairdryer. Have the hairdryer on a cool setting and keep it moving, as it can melt the polyester mesh if trained on one area too long. Mix the next colour and print the second layer. John is using the one-arm squeegee holder rather than pulling by hand.

7. Stack the prints on the rack to dry. They may take a little longer this time, since the paper has been sealed by the first layer of colour and the ink cannot sink into it. Clean and dry the screen *in situ*. Repeat the process of putting the master drawing underneath and painting out any areas that you want to stay the second colour.

8. Set up and print the third colour. The picture shows the third colour layer drying on the rack.

9. Continue in this way until you feel that your print is complete. In this instance, there was only one more layer of black. The following illustrations show the picture as it builds up in colour layers.

OPPOSITE AND ABOVE: **The print building up and the final version.**

To clean the screen when you have finished your print, first wash off as much ink as possible and remove all of the tape from the edges. Wearing rubber gloves and an apron, prop the screen in a suitable sink or washout trough, or even do this outside if necessary. Using a brush or pad coat both sides of the screen with the stencil remover solution. Wait for 3–4 minutes for the solution to do its work. Check that the stencil is beginning to break down before you start spraying (you should see it literally beginning to run down the screen). Then spray, close to, from the flat side of the screen so that you do not get splashed when the water hits the screen frame. With hand-painted stencils, where the stencil may be of variable thickness or may have a dried film of ink covering it in parts, you might have to do this more than once to get the screen thoroughly clean. Hold it up to the light and check for tiny bits of stencil that you might have missed the first time around.

CHAPTER 5

DRAWING FLUID AND FILLER STENCILS

This is yet another low-tech way of working directly on to a screen to make a stencil. It can easily be used at home, in an artist's studio, or in a school, since it does not require access to specialist equipment. It is a painterly way of working, which, unlike the reductive method described in Chapter 4, allows you to make a positive image. When using screen filler on its own, you paint out what you do not want to print, so in effect you are working in negative. With drawing fluid, you are painting what you do want to print, so it is a positive way of working.

There are several varieties of fluid and filler on the market made by different manufacturers, but they all work in a similar way. The one used in this example is made by Speedball, but Daler-Rowney, Jacquard, Lascaux and others all make their own versions and each will supply specific instructions on cleaning up and recycling the screens using their products.

The system works by using a soluble drawing medium, a water-based fluid, to draw or paint the image on to the screen. Once this is dry, the unpainted areas are blocked out with a screen filler, which, when dry, is water resistant. The original drawing is then washed out with water, leaving the water-resistant filler behind to form the stencil.

It is a simple and direct process that can be used very expressively. You can be inventive in the ways that you apply the drawing fluid, from painting it on with different brushes, to stippling, stamping, sponging, scraping and stencilling to create a variety of marks and textures.

Materials and equipment

- screen with an open area masked out to the required size and with the edges taped ready for use (*see* Chapter 3)
- screen filler and drawing fluid
- selection of brushes and other implements of your choice for applying the drawing fluid
- hairdryer to speed up the drying process
- scraper (cardboard or old store card) for applying filler
- newspapers
- paper
- inks for printing
- squeegee
- cold water and a sponge or rag
- nylon bristle brush (washing-up brush or similar)
- protective gloves
- recommended cleaner for your screen filler, or a weak solution of washing soda (made up from soda crystals)
- garden hose with a spray or pressure wash for recycling the screen.

Method

In the following step-by-step example, artist Frances Quail experiments with the medium to make her first ever screenprint.

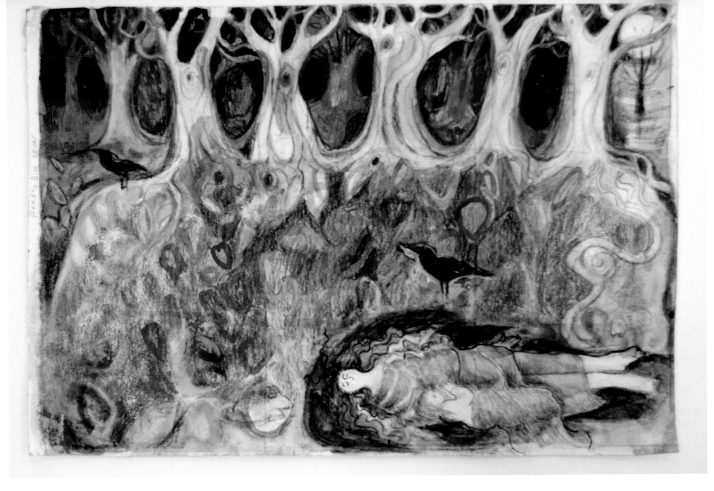

1a. The starting point for the print is a watercolour sketch created as an illustration.

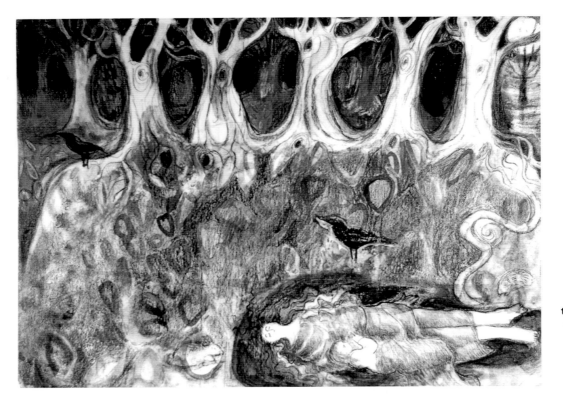

1b. This was copied and enlarged as a black and white image to act as the master drawing. The idea was not to try to re-create the original watercolour, but to use it as a starting point to explore the potential of the medium and learn how to translate from one medium into another.

2. Mask out (using screen filler) an open area on the screen that is the same size as the master drawing (as in Chapter 3). Alternatively, if you have access to the equipment, as we did here, make a photostencil using a piece of black cartridge paper as the positive (*see* Chapter 7 on photostencils). Position the open screen over the master drawing and prop it up with something fairly thin at all four corners so that it does not rest directly on the image. This is to prevent the drawing fluid from coming into contact with the image underneath and sticking to it.

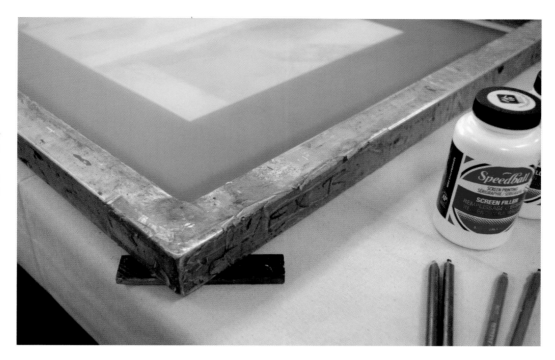

3. Using the master image as a guide, paint everything that you want to print in the first colour with drawing fluid, then dry it with a hairdryer on a cool setting, taking care not to scorch the mesh. You may find it helpful to trace parts of the drawing on to the screen with a soft pencil first.

4. Using a scraper (such as an old store card or similar), thinly cover the entire painting with the screen filler. Hold the scraper at right angles to the screen mesh so that you are not 'squishing' the filler through to the other side of the mesh and making the layer of filler too thick. Then dry with a hairdryer on a cool setting. Be aware that the fillers are designed to do their job remarkably well, so they do not need to be put on thickly; also that they are water-resistant, so the thicker they are, the more difficult it will be to clean the stencil off after use.

5. Put the dried screen on a pad of newspaper and wash out the drawing fluid with cold water and a sponge or rag, leaving the screen filler behind to form the stencil. Dry the screen again.

6. The finished stencil. After taping up the edges in the usual way, the screen is ready to print.

7. The stencil printed in cyan blue. After printing the first colour, the screen can be recycled, leaving the outside stencil mostly intact if possible.

8a. In a suitable sink or trough, using a nylon bristle brush or pad, coat the screen filler with washing-soda solution, or the manufacturer's recommended cleaner. Scrub all over on both sides of the screen. Leave the screen to rest in a horizontal position for a few minutes to allow the solution to penetrate the stencil.

8b. Spray off the stencil vigorously using a hose with a spray attachment or a pressure washer. You may need to scrub some more to help it along.

9 Dry the screen and you are ready to repeat the whole procedure to make the next colour layer. There is no limit to the number of layers that you can use to get closer to the result you want, except for your ingenuity and patience. You may make decisions as you progress, rather than plan the whole image beforehand.

The completed print with many transparent colour layers.

CHAPTER 6

MONOPRINTING THROUGH THE SCREEN

A monoprint by definition is a one-off print that cannot be repeated. It is a painterly method of working that is essentially simple, but requires some spontaneity and speed. In the step-by-step example shown here, painter/photographer Annie Mendelow works directly on to an open screen using water-based pastel, brushes and acrylic paint mixed with screen-printing medium. Annie often works from the life model or still life and has based her monoprints on pastel drawings.

Materials and equipment

- some images for inspiration (Annie worked from photos of her work on her iPad)
- screen with an open area masked out to the required size and with the edges taped ready for use (*see* Chapter 3)
- water-soluble pastels
- selection of colours to work with, either acrylic paint mixed with screen-printing medium or readymade water-based screen-printing inks preferably mixed with some extra acrylic retarder to slow down the drying time
- brush for each colour; stiff hog-hair brushes are easier to work with and it is good to have a selection of sizes and shapes
- squeegee
- card for scraping up excess ink
- bucket and sponge for cleaning.

1. Materials.

Method

1 Set the open screen up on the table ready to print with the registration stops in place (*see* Chapter 3). Get everything ready before you start; once there is ink in the screen you need to work fast. Very lightly, dampen the image area with clean water.

2 Roughly sketch out the image on the screen using a water-soluble pastel.

3 Prop up the screen with a suitable prop to stop the ink from getting all over the table.

2. Pastel drawing on screen.

3 BELOW. Screen propped on roll of masking tape.

4 BELOW RIGHT. Painting on screen.

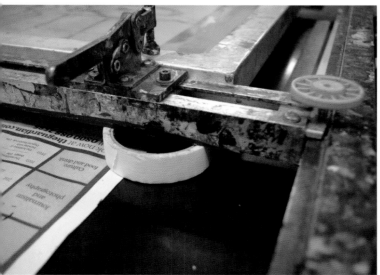

4 Begin painting directly onto the screen, working rapidly.

5 You can redefine your image at any time using the pastels. Dip them in water first before you draw.

RIGHT AND BELOW:
5. Dip pastel in water.

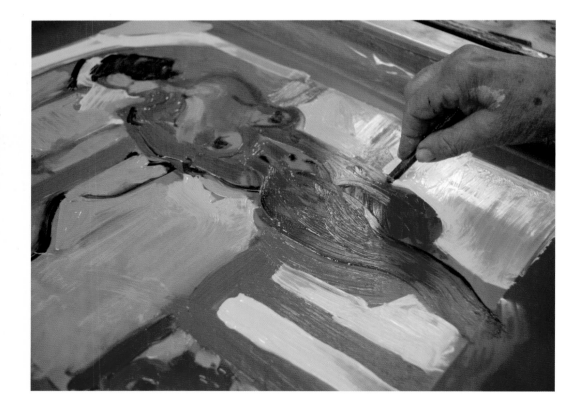

6 When you have more or less filled the entire print area (this means that the image will not move with the squeegee and streak when printing), dribble a bead of screen-printing medium along the top edge of the image. The medium is used on its own without colour and is there to help the squeegee slide across the painted image smoothly.

6. Dribble a bead along the top edge.

7 Pull the print holding the squeegee at the usual 45-degree angle until you are past the end of the image.

8 You will end up with a streaky muddle of ink at the bottom of the screen.

Scrape this up and put it in a spare pot.

7a & b. Pull the print.

8a ABOVE: **Scrape up the excess ink.**

8b. Pot of excess streaky ink.

9 Put your print on the rack to dry and swiftly begin work on
the next one.

9a. Freshly pulled print.

9b OPPOSITE. **The finished monoprint.**

10a ABOVE. **More prints from the same session.**

10b. **Another from the same session.**

10 There will be the ghost of the image visible in the screen, so, if you wish, you can make another similar version by repainting. In this way, it is possible to create a variable series of images that explore the same themes or colours.

11 After a while, things can build up and get messy. Eventually the screen will dry in places and the colours will become murky, so it is a good idea to scrape up and wash the screen down periodically, so that you can start again.

You can also monoprint with water-soluble pastels on their own. Dip them in water before you draw and use them with care, as occasionally they have gritty lumps of pigment in them that can pop a screen mesh if you rub too hard. Water-soluble crayons work too, as do watercolour paints. Even soft pencil (such as 6B) or graphite drawn on to the screen will print. Just use the clear screen-printing medium to print them down on to the paper. With a harder medium like pencil, it may take several pulls to get everything printed satisfactorily and care must be taken not to damage the screen mesh as you draw.

You can also build up the images by working into them several times, allowing them to dry on the rack in-between layers. In this sense, monoprinting through the screen is no different to painting or drawing. Many artists find that the limitations of painting through the screen help to make them more decisive, which in turn reflects back into their other artwork.

Yet another refinement of the monoprint process is to use blends of colour through the screen. This is where you have, in its simplest form, one colour at one end of the squeegee and another at the other end. After a few pulls, the colours begin to mix and soften on the screen. Rather than stay in bold stripes, they gradually blend together to form a smooth gradient. Blends are fun and very useful for introducing tonal variations into your work. They can also be combined with other stencil-making techniques to create complex illusions. However, they can only be printed in the direction of the pull and keeping them in place throughout an edition is a skilful business that takes practice.

Another fine creative mess.

A colour blend on the screen.

Printing the blend.

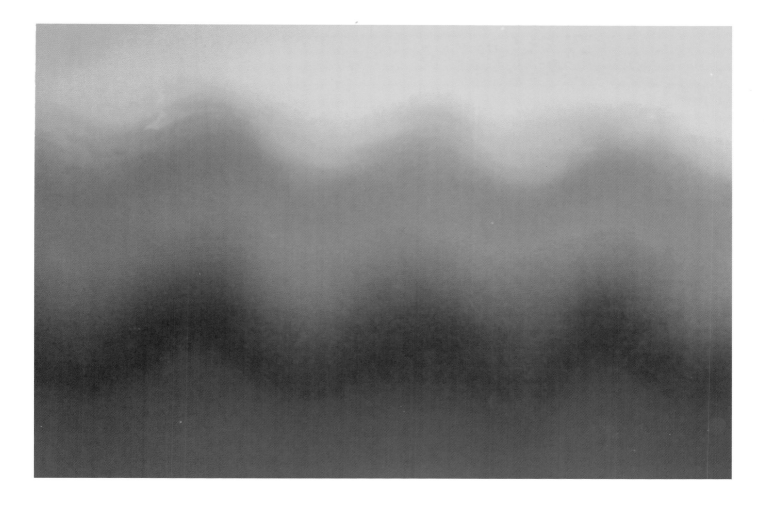

It is also possible to flood a blend across a screen while moving the squeegee to make curved blends. You can experiment with both this and the possible colour changes to your heart's content – it can be very addictive!

CHAPTER 7

PHOTOGRAPHIC STENCIL MAKING – THE BASICS

Making up the photoemulsion

Direct emulsion (that is not an SBQ) comes in two parts, a base emulsion and a sensitizer. The sensitizer is provided in a dark-coloured bottle and usually consists of a powder that needs to be dissolved by filling the sensitizer bottle with warm water and shaking it up. Take care when handling the sensitizer, as it has a powerful yellow stain. If you don't want to look like a heavy smoker, wear gloves.

Make sure that the screen you are using is thoroughly clean and dry. Hold it up to the light and scan the mesh, looking for blocked areas. Screens will inevitably get stained with use, but stains are not usually a problem until you can't see through them and they start 'ghosting' back, at which point you will need to clean the screen, after removing the stencil, with a special dehazing product (*see* Chapter 2).

Coating a screen with direct emulsion

This should really be carried out in a room with gold or red safety lighting, although it can also be done in subdued daylight or artificial light, provided that there is no direct sunlight anywhere near the screen. Once coated, however, the screen must be dried in the dark, preferably flat rather than upright, with the flat side facing downwards. This may seem counter-intuitive, but drying the screen with the flat side down allows most of the emulsion to sink through to the back of the screen. Having a thicker coating on the flat side of the screen (the side that goes down on to the paper) gives the stencil a sharper, cleaner edge and therefore a crisper print.

Drying the screen upright will allow the emulsion to slide towards the ground. The resulting stencil will be thinner at the top than the bottom, making the exposure uneven. These differences are small and probably would not bother most occasional printers, but they can make a difference when exposing detail. You are aiming to get a thin, even coating on to both sides of your screen.

Materials and equipment

- coating trough
- photoemulsion
- heated drying cabinet or a dark cupboard with a source of warmth (such as a fan heater on a cool setting)
- old store card or similar for scraping the emulsion back into the storage pot
- an exposure unit or other UV light source
- a washout trough or similar where the screen can be propped and washed out
- pressure washer or garden hose with a jet spray attachment.

Method

1 Fill a coating trough, which is the right length to fit within the screen frame, two-thirds full with photoemulsion. It is very difficult to coat a screen successfully without a coating trough, although many have tried. The trough needs to fit inside the frame comfortably. Ideally, it will be a centimetre or two shorter than the inside measurement of the frame. Remember to replace the lid on the pot of emulsion, especially if you are not using safety lighting.

2 Hold or prop the clean, dry screen at a slight angle, with the flat side facing you ready for coating. You can hold the screen yourself and coat one-handed, or use both hands and get someone else to hold the screen for you. Alternatively, it can be propped against a wall with a plank of wood at the bottom against which to rest the lower edge, so that it will not slip away from you when pressure is applied.

RIGHT: **Someone holding the screen for you.**

Propping it against a wall.

3 Start at the bottom of the screen, making sure that the emulsion is level in the trough. Tip the trough slightly and wait until all of the emulsion has made contact with the screen.

4 With steady, even pressure, tip the trough a little more and draw it up the screen without straying on to the frame. If you stray on to the frame, you will end up with a thick patch of emulsion in those places. At about 5cm from the top, stop and, without taking any pressure off, tip the trough back slightly and scoop to fill the last bit of mesh. In this way, you will not end up with a thick line of emulsion at the top of the screen, or spread emulsion all over the frame.

Thick lines of emulsion will take a long time to dry and be more difficult to remove when recycling the screen later on. For this reason, check the edges of the coating and wipe off any thick lines and also any dribbles, because these will drip inside the drying cabinet, if you are using one, probably on to another screen.

If it has not gone perfectly and your coating is too thick or patchy in places, all is not lost. You can use the edge of the coating trough, without tipping it enough to get more emulsion on to the screen, to scrape off the excess and even out the coating. However, you do need to scrape the whole thing, starting right from the bottom again, or lines will be left in the coating.

5 Repeat this procedure on the other side of the screen.

6 Slot the screen into the drying cabinet with its flat side down.

It should take around 15–20min to dry properly in a heated cabinet. If you are using a DIY approach, make sure that the heat source is not too hot, as excessive heat will set the emulsion. Also ensure that the screen is completely protected from light as it dries.

7 Scrape the leftover photoemulsion back into the pot as soon as possible, especially if you are not doing this in safe light. Wash the trough and end caps with cold running water, paying particular attention to the edge of the trough and the grooves in the end caps.

Exposing a screen

This process is going to vary depending upon the type of exposure unit that you are using. On a standard unit, you would place the positive reading correctly, emulsion side up, on to the glass of the print-down frame and place the screen flat side down on top of it. The rule is to have the emulsion side of the film in direct contact with the emulsion on the screen, so that there is no intervening layer of film. If it is a handmade positive, the emulsion side is the side that the drawing is on.

Turn on the vacuum and wait until all of the air between the glass and the rubber lid has been drawn out, then make a timed exposure. Make sure that the glass is as clean and free of dust as possible, so as to avoid having to spot out pinholes in the stencil

Screen being coated.

caused by dust particles. You could try making two exposures of half the required length, moving the screen after the first exposure so that dust and scratches will be in a different place. If you do this, the positive will need to be taped on to the screen to make sure that it does not move when the vacuum is released.

Calculating exposure times

The power of the light source, the distance of this from the stencil and the speed of the emulsion will all make a significant difference to the length of time it will take to harden. The mesh you are using will also have an impact. A coarse mesh will hold more emulsion and make a much thicker stencil that will take longer to expose than a thinner stencil on a finer mesh.

What the positive is made of is also important. For example, if you are using a photocopy on thin paper as your positive, the light will take a long time to penetrate through the paper to set the emulsion and it will need a much longer exposure. A film positive would be much faster.

With experience, you can make an educated guess and use a bit of trial and error to calculate the optimum timing. However, sometimes it is hard to know where to start, so in the beginning it is useful to use an exposure calculator. You can buy or download several versions of one of these from specialist trade suppliers such as MacDermid Autotype or Ulano.

In the Autotype example, there are five identical positives laid out as columns. Four of these have been backed with a neutral

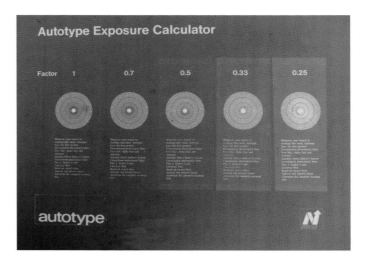

Exposed screen using an Autotype calculator.

grey filter of a different density, which cuts down the amount of light that can get through. This is the equivalent of cutting down the exposure time and is expressed as a factor – 0.25, for example. To use the calculator, make an educated guess at the amount of time needed, then double it. Expose, wash out and dry your photostencil in the normal way, then look at the result. There will be a colour change from one column to the next, going from light to dark.

The column where this colour change stops is the one that has had optimum exposure. Read the factor for this column

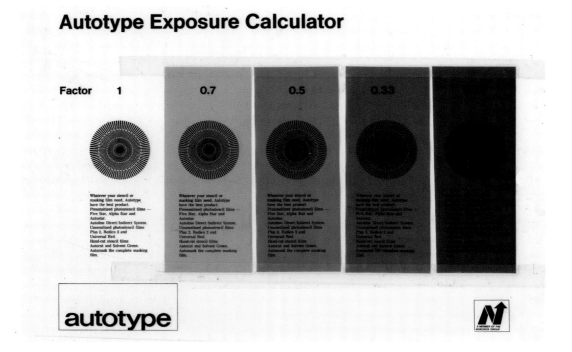

MacDermid Autotype exposure calculator.

and multiply it by your original (guessed and doubled) exposure time – the resulting figure will be the correct exposure. In the example shown, the colour change stops at factor 0.7; the doubled exposure guess was 60sec. The correct exposure is therefore 0.7 × 60sec = 42sec. This type of exposure calculator allows you to evaluate the equivalent of several different exposure times in one hit and saves a lot of time and effort.

It is possible to make your own simple test-exposure calculator using the type of positive material that you will be working with. The example shown here was made in Photoshop using concentric rings, a bitmap (diffusion dither), straight lines and some halftone. This homemade positive can be exposed in 10sec steps, covering less of the positive at each step with black paper. The circles in my version helped to position the paper at regular intervals. In this way, one strip on the screen will have had only 10sec exposure, while its neighbour will have had 20sec and so on. Once the screen is exposed, washed and dried, it is easy to spot at which point the emulsion stopped changing colour, meaning that optimum exposure has taken place. In this case, it was at 40sec.

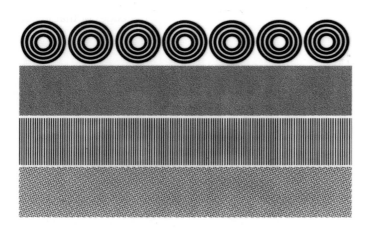

Homemade positive.

Stepped exposures.

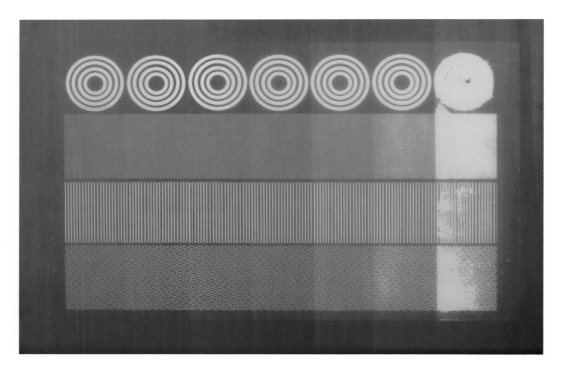

Exposed homemade version on screen.

Washing out

After the exposure, the stencil must be washed out straight away. Spray both sides of the screen all over with the cold water spray or pressure washer before concentrating on the image. It is important to wash the whole stencil to remove any unhardened emulsion. As the screen is drying after washout, its dampness may act like a capillary mat, carrying unexposed emulsion into open areas and forming a silvery deposit or scum. This most often accumulates at the very edges of an image and can be difficult to spot. Thorough washing will alleviate this potential problem. Do most of the washing, however, from the flat side of the screen, as this is the side that has received the most light and will therefore be the toughest. Do not spray too closely until you are sure that the stencil is strong enough to take it and keep the spray moving.

Troubleshooting

Underexposure

If the stencil starts washing off completely, either the exposure has been too short, or the coating has been too thick or uneven in those places. If the surface of the emulsion on the inside (squeegee side) of the screen feels slimy, it is possible that the exposure has been too short and washing too much on this side of the screen can result in a thin stencil with lots of pinholes. If not washed out properly, it will tend to scum. An underexposed screen will also be more difficult to decoat afterwards.

Hold the screen up to the light, or turn on the backlight if you have one and carefully look the stencil over, as it is easy to miss fine details. When you are happy that it is clear, blot the excess water out of the stencil either with newsprint or with a damp chamois leather made into a pad. Work from the flat side of the screen; the other side will sometimes still be slightly sticky. Blotting helps to stop scum from forming, as does force-drying the screen in a drying cabinet, or with a fan heater on the cool setting.

Overexposure

It is not possible to overexpose the photoemulsion, since it sets and then goes no further. It is, however, possible to overexpose a positive that is not quite lightproof.

So if you have lost detail then it is likely to be a combination of overexposure and a bad positive.

Multiple positives

If using multiple positives, it is important to work out how best to position them by thinking ahead to the printing stage. It is common for people to cram as many images into one screen as possible in the mistaken belief that this will save time, effort and money. It usually doesn't – most often you just give yourself a whole load of technical problems when printing. Below are a few 'rules' to follow when using multiple positives.

Rule 1   Position multiple positives far enough apart so that you can mask them off easily without the tape getting in the way of the squeegee. A lump of tape next to an image can make all the difference as to whether the edges of that image print well or not.

Rule 2   Leave at least a 5cm border at the sides of the screen when printing on paper. This is because of the snap-off between the mesh and the tabletop. Where the mesh is glued to the frame the tension is very tight, so it is not possible to stretch the mesh enough to make contact with the table underneath and therefore the corresponding edges will not print properly. Also, you risk tearing your expensive mesh.

Rule 3   Leave at least 10–12cm top and bottom if pulling the squeegee by hand, or at the sides if using a one arm. At the top, there needs to be room for the ink to lie and for the squeegee to rest, or the ink will start dripping through the open areas of the stencil. When printing, you need to hold the squeegee at an angle of 45 degrees. If you do not have enough space at the end of the pull to keep it at this angle (because you are going to hit the side of the frame), then the bottom of the image will not print cleanly.

Rule 4   Think about the printing order and position the positives accordingly.

Rule 5   Awkward printing positions are no fun. Having to lean over one image to print another that has been positioned above it on the screen is sometimes tricky.

You could try having your positives pointing in opposing directions and turning the screen round on the table halfway through, so that the image that you want to print is always the one closest to you and is always the right way up.

Notes on setting up and printing

Check your dried screen up against the light and search for pinholes. Bits of dust on the exposure unit can cause these.

Spot them out with screen filler. If using a brush for this, wash it immediately afterwards, as the screen filler is water-resistant once dry.

The screen will leak around the edges where there is a gap between the stencil and the frame. Mask out this gap with vinyl packing tape. Ordinary packing tape, although cheaper, will leave its glue behind when you strip it off prior to recycling the screen, making your job that much harder. It is worth paying for better quality tape. The tape should cover the gap between the stencil and the screen frame and also go up the side of the frame. This makes cleaning up easier and stops your frames from getting covered in hardened ink over time.

Mixing ink

Acrylic paint dries really fast, so when using it for printing a retardant needs to be added to slow down the drying time. This is sold in the form of screen-printing medium. Acrylic paint does not really have the right consistency to print with and is quite opaque. The screen-printing medium that is added to the paint serves three purposes:

- It slows down the drying time.
- It gives the right flowing consistency for printing.
- It makes colours more transparent.

Translucent colour layers often look more aesthetically pleasing than opaque ones – they glow more because the white paper can shine through and beautiful overprints can be achieved (where one colour crosses over another to create a third over-printed colour). Overprints can sometimes be very unpredictable – practice and experience are the key to using colour effectively. Remember that physical pigment on paper does not always behave in the same way as the colours that appear on a computer screen.

Adjusting the snap-off

When you are printing on paper (as opposed to fabric), there should be a small gap between the screen and the tabletop. This gap is called snap-off and it needs to be there, otherwise the paper will simply stick to the ink in the screen as you pull the squeegee across, particularly when printing a large, flat area of colour. The idea is to hold the squeegee at an angle of around 45 degrees as you do the pull. This angle means that only the sharp edge of the blade is in contact with the paper underneath and the screen can snap-off on either side of the blade.

If you are holding the squeegee too flat or too high, the paper will stick to the screen and you will either smudge the print whilst pulling it off, or it will drop off slowly, creating swirl marks. These will show in the print, especially if you are using a translucent colour. This is not true of printing on fabric, which is absorbent and usually glued or pinned down to the tabletop and therefore is unlikely to stick. When printing on fabric, you can have the screen in direct contact with the fabric surface.

Snap-off is easy to adjust. On a professional screen-printing bed designed for paper, there is a screw mechanism on all four corners of the frame that holds the screen, which allows it to be raised or lowered. The amount that you need to raise or lower the frame is usually very small; tiny adjustments can make all the difference as to how well the image prints and whether it sticks or not. At the front of the table, the mechanism is a simple screw. At the back, where counterbalance weights are usually attached, the mechanism is still a screw, but it has to be much

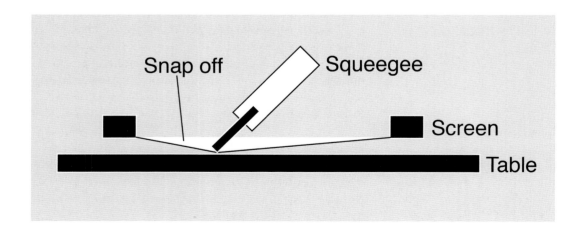

Snap-off diagram.

Registration diagram.

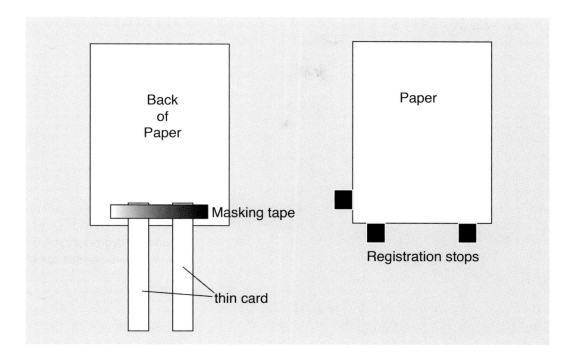

more robust to carry the weight and often has a small wheel attached to help you turn it.

On a homemade set-up, the width (in cross-section) of the hinges or jiffy clamps that you are using should give you enough snap at the top (back edge) of the screen. However, you may need to tape a couple of bits of card to the front edge to give it enough lift.

It is always good practice to do a test print on to rough paper (called a printout) before you start your run on good paper. Then you can check that the screen snaps off nicely. You should see the screen following the blade, snapping off in a neat curve. If, for example, it sticks on one side more than another, that side of the frame probably needs to be raised very slightly. Conversely, it is also possible to have too much snap. This will stop the squeegee blade from making proper contact with the paper and table underneath and will prevent you from printing down the edges of your print successfully.

Registration

In order to get one colour layer of a print to align with the next, there needs to be a system of registration. Every print has to go down in the same position on every sheet of paper, even on the first colour layer, otherwise you will not be able to register subsequent layers successfully. Even if you do not intend to print many prints or many layers, registration using register stops is a good habit to get into.

When screenprinting on a flatbed, this is done by moving the paper into position under the screen, rather than moving the screen around to align with the print, then marking one corner and edge of the paper with lays or registration stops that are stuck down on to the tabletop. You need three registration stops, a fancy name for bits of paper or thin card stuck down in position with masking or double-sided tape. The card should be just thick enough to make a positive bump against which to place your paper, but not so thick that it sticks up beyond it and gets in the way of the squeegee as it passes over.

Position the paper under the screen once it is set up on the table. While the screen is still clean, you will be able to see where the image will come out on the paper beneath by looking through the mesh. If you want to be more accurate, you can mark up, on one sheet of the printing paper, where you want the image to come out. Or, if you have made your screen from a positive, stick the relevant positive in the correct position to one of your prints and use this under the screen. Since the positive is a dark colour, it can be seen clearly through the mesh. To make things easier, thin card arms can be attached to one sheet of paper to enable you to position it without having to keep raising the screen. When you are happy with the position, use two register stops on one corner and a third on one edge of the paper, as in the diagram above. If using masking tape, make sure that it comes right up to the edge of the stop, so that the paper will not slide underneath.

It is always useful to mark where you positioned the registration stops on a few excess prints. These will be your registration copies for future layers. All printers, no matter how experienced, rely on having waste copies to use for registration and colour testing.

Be warned, however, that registering by looking through the screen is not always a completely accurate way of positioning when printing on paper because of the distance (snap-off) between the screen and the tabletop. This small gap means that the screen has to stretch slightly to make contact with the paper beneath and in doing so can fractionally shift the actual print in the direction of the pull. This slight shift can easily be corrected on a bed with precise registration after the first registration print has been looked at for reference.

Where the registration is particularly tricky and where there is no precise registration to use, it is practical to use a sheet of acetate, or something similar, firmly attached to the print table using a hinge of masking tape. The acetate needs to be clean, flat and larger than the print area and the paper in order to work successfully. Print the new image on to the sheet of acetate first, then slide the sheet of paper (with the first printed colour layer) under the acetate and line up the two images. When you are happy with the position, fold the acetate out of the way, allowing it to hang over the edge of the table on its makeshift hinge (*see* Chapter 3). It is useful to keep it there for reference should things go awry. Stick the register stops to the table as before, using the same corner and edge. This is where your register copies and their marks come in handy. Remember that if you change the corner or edge at which you are registering, the registration will not always be the same and things can start to go wrong.

Printing

The flood stroke

Pour a line of ink on to the screen along the bottom edge of the image. Make sure that the line of ink goes the full length of the squeegee blade so that it has something to slide on. Lift the screen with one hand while holding the squeegee with the other. Flood the screen with ink by pushing the roll of ink away from you, holding the squeegee at an angle of around 45 degrees. The angle of the blade is critical – you need to use the sharp edge to get a good flood. Put a little pressure on, so that you get a good, clean, even fill. Try to avoid taking the ink right

up to the top of the screen and on to the frame. This is where you will rest the squeegee when it is not being used. This will stop ink from getting all over the squeegee handle, then on to your hands and anything else that you touch.

A good, even flood will give you a good, even print. If the flood stroke is bad, then the print will also be bad, because it is the ink in the mesh that hits the paper, not the ink that you pull down over the top of it. If you run out of ink or have to flood several times, the layer of ink in the mesh will be uneven and the print quality will be affected.

The pull

Lay the screen down in place. Position your squeegee behind the roll of ink using both hands this time. Make contact with the tabletop underneath before you start the pull, holding the squeegee at the critical 45-degree angle so that you use only the sharpest edge of the blade. Pull the roll of ink over the flooded image; the screen should snap-off as you do so. This means that the paper is not sticking to the back of the screen. If the paper does stick then:

- You have forgotten to turn the vacuum on, or (on a homemade bench) the spray glue needs refreshing.
- The ink mix is too thick and sticky.
- There is not enough snap-off between the screen mesh and the tabletop.
- You are holding the squeegee at the wrong angle.
- A combination of the above.

Raise the screen and check that the print is okay. If there are missing bits, you can pull again as long as the paper has not moved. In this case, do not reflood the screen. Just pull the print again, concentrating on printing down the missing bits. When all is correct, reflood ready for the next print. It is best to leave a screen flooded between prints, because the ink will not dry in the mesh so fast. Leave the squeegee parked at the top of the screen in its groove (in the handle) to prevent the squeegee from falling off when you lift the screen.

Raise the screen, retrieve the print and put it on the rack to dry. Position the next sheet of paper carefully up against the stops and print the rest of the run. It is customary to stack prints in the rack with their ends sticking out slightly beyond the tray. This makes it much easier and faster to remove the prints when they are dry. When you have printed the last print, do not reflood, so as to make it easier to clean up.

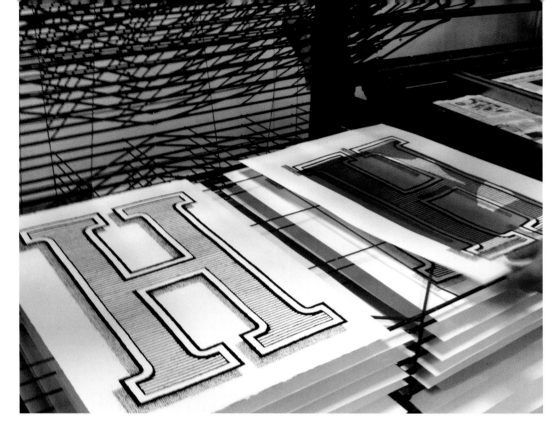

Stack of prints drying in the rack.

Cleaning up

At the table

There are some instances when it is preferable to clean the screen at the table rather than removing it to a sink or wash-room. If you are doing the former, place some newspaper under the screen so as to keep the table clean. You will need a bucket of cold water and a sponge or rag. Scrape up as much ink as possible and put it back in the pot, as it can be used again. If kept covered, it will last a long time, although it may need a drop of water and/or screen medium to revitalize it. Wash the top surface of the screen thoroughly, changing the water and rinsing out the sponge or rag frequently.

When the top surface is as clean as you can get it, rinse out the sponge and 'polish' the image area from underneath. This vital 'polish' is the one that really cleans out the image area. You can use a hairdryer to speed things up, but be careful not to scorch the mesh – use a cool setting and keep the draught of air from the hairdryer moving. The screen needs to be dry before you can print through it again and so does your print, so now is the time to plan your next layer, mix your next colour, or take a break.

If you want to get good prints, it is essential to keep the screen as clean as possible and not allow ink to dry in the mesh. Acrylic is very tough when dry and difficult to remove without resorting to caustic-based cleaners or solvents. For this reason, it is advisable to clean the ink out of a screen as soon as possible after printing.

Removing a stencil

Wash the ink off the screen and remove any tape, as these will get in the way of the stencil remover. If there is a dried film of acrylic ink over the stencil, try using a kitchen cleaner (containing quaternary ammonium compounds rather than bleach) to break it down first. But make sure that you are working in a well-ventilated area if you do this.

In a suitable trough and wearing proper protection (fully protective gloves, an apron and eye protection), apply stencil remover to both sides of the screen using a soft brush or pad, making sure that the stencil is covered right up to the edges. Give it 3–4min to start working. It is best to keep brushing until you can visibly see signs that the emulsion is breaking down and running off the screen. Then, wearing ear protection, spray with the pressure washer on the flat side of the screen. On this side, the water jet will not hit the side of the frame and spray back at you, splattering you with photoemulsion.

Hold the water jet very close to the screen mesh and keep it moving. The stencil should come off easily. If it does not, you probably did not leave it long enough before spraying and you will need another application of stencil remover. If you do not possess a pressure washer, a garden spray will do, but you may need to scrub a bit more with the brush to get rid of stubborn bits. Examine the clean screen up against a light source to make sure that you have not missed anything.

Warning Do not leave stencil remover on for too long, as the stencil will start to break down and then dry out again, locking it on to the mesh so firmly that it will be very difficult to remove.

CHAPTER 8

MAKING POSITIVES FOR PHOTOSTENCILS

In screenprinting, a positive is something that will block ultra-violet light and is carried on a translucent support. This chapter explores a number of different ways to make successful positives by hand. Chapter 9 is dedicated to making digital positives.

Daisy Daisy by Rachel Brookes-Read. Hand-cut black paper positives have been used to expose two layers of colour.

Photoemulsion coated on a screen behaves in a simple fashion. Either it sets or it doesn't, depending upon whether it is exposed to enough ultraviolet light or not. Likewise, the stencil created on the screen is very simple. Either there are open areas of mesh that allow the ink to pass through, or the mesh is blocked by hardened photoemulsion.

If you shy away from using the computer, or do not have access to the necessary software, it is perfectly possible to create positives by hand. In some instances, to achieve certain visual effects, it would also be more desirable. Working by hand introduces the possibility of accidental discovery, or the beauty of chance in a physical way that can be missing from digital work. To be able to combine the best aspects of both methods is even more interesting. One of the most attractive things about silkscreenprinting is its ability to 'collage' disparate images, marks and media together into one satisfying whole. Photo silkscreen allows you to do this in abundance.

Black paper

The simplest positive of all is a sheet of black paper, most often used as the cheapest way to create a background or solid block of colour. However, interesting positives can be made simply by paper cutting. This is just like using a paper stencil, only with the added advantage of durability. The possibilities are endless including the laser-cut route.

Hand-cut black paper positive.

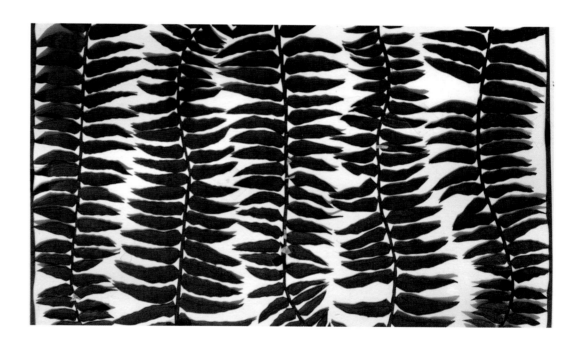

Print from the positive with a colour blend printed underneath it.

Red or amber film

This is a specially manufactured film for making hand-cut positives. It consists of a layer of coloured film supported on an acetate backing. The coloured layer can be peeled away from the acetate, leaving the acetate untouched so that it holds the floating parts of the design together in the correct position. It has been around since the days that a positive was produced in a photographic darkroom using a process camera and developing the film in trays of developer and fixer.

The amber or red colour blocks ultraviolet light, but has the added advantage of being translucent. Many layers of the film can be placed on top of one another on a lightbox, making the registration of different-coloured layers easy to see and therefore more accurate. To achieve a good result takes a very sharp scalpel or swivel knife and a light touch, so mastery of this technique takes a bit of practice, although minor mistakes can be fixed by reapplying some of the material that has been peeled off.

The coloured layers underneath the final black key line would deliberately be cut slightly too large, so that the black layer would overlap them when it is printed, thus avoiding little white lines showing at the edges. In printer's speak, this is called a 'bleed'. Computer users would call it 'trapping'.

Cutting amber film.

Using found objects

You can use found objects as your positives provided that they block the light. Anything that is flat without any protrusions that will deform the screen mesh or damage the glass and neoprene of a print down frame can be used. Things like leaves and dried plant matter will make great silhouettes for example. Once you start looking there are possibilities everywhere.

LEFT: **Card printed from amber film layers.**

OPPOSITE: ***Spider Gloves* by Jane Sampson. Screenprint exposed from stockings and gloves (2005).**

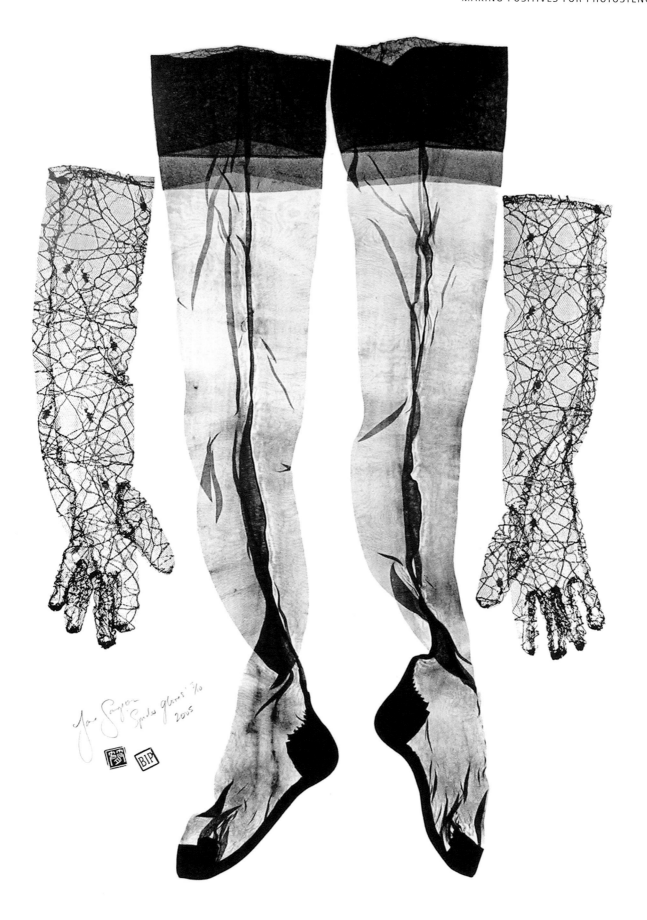

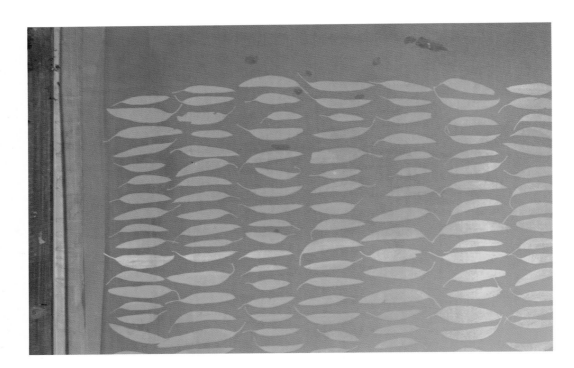

Detail of screen exposed using eucalyptus leaves.

Cloth or clothing, for example, can be exploited for its texture, shape and form. In the past, I have used underwear, lace, scarves, blackened etching scrim (a loosely woven fabric), threads and wool (mohair is particularly good), ribbons, pom-poms, feather boas, dried plants and even a mophead, as my drawing tools to create positives. This is the ultimate photogram.

The detail that you can achieve from the right object can be amazing, although finding the right exposure time will require some trial and error. This is not an exact science and some things work better at blocking the light than others. Folds and creases will just come out as silhouettes, for example.

Hand-rendered positives

Simple black and white positives can be drawn or painted on to tracing paper, acetate, drafting film, or even very thin paper with a variety of pens, pencils and inks. Exposure times will need to be adjusted to compensate for the nature of the chosen substrate. Thin paper will take significantly longer to expose than acetate, for example.

Exposing a piece of scrim in the printdown frame.

ABOVE: **Textural detail of the resulting scrim print.**

Print made using a feather boa, buttons, wire and ribbon.

Drafting film and a selection of drawing materials.

PREVIOUS PAGE: *Buka* **by Anita Bernaka.**

BELOW RIGHT: **The sequence of prints showing the build-up of drawn layers.**

What you draw or paint with is important. Lines drawn with felt-tips and drawing pens that have a blue cast when looked at on a lightbox will not be effective, since blue does not block ultraviolet light. Red, however, does, so any pens that have a distinctly brown or reddish cast will probably work. Chalk pens such as the Posca and Zig brands are ideal. They come in many different widths, just like felt-tips, but they block the light really well. Indian ink, Rotring ink and black acrylic paint are all good, as is Photopaque, a red sticky liquid made with powdered terracotta that is used for spotting out negatives. Liquid media may not stick well to acetate or drafting film. The addition of some PVA or washing-up liquid (in very tiny amounts) will help to break the surface tension and allow the drawing or painting media to lie flat and stick to non-absorbent surfaces.

The print *Buka* was hand-drawn from an original sketch on to drafting film by artist Anita Bernaka using Posca pens. She drew each new layer that corresponded to each colour on a new piece of drafting film. While editioning the print, we kept back one of each colour layer to illustrate how the print was built up layer by layer.

The print contained no tonal elements and each layer of flat colour built up on the last, taking advantage of the fact that screen inks can be mixed opaquely enough to cover the colour underneath. This avoided the need for 'butt' registration, where one colour butts up against another and thus the possibility of white lines where the layers are misaligned.

Hand-rendered positives using mark resist

Drafting film and acetate are not capable of holding much in the way of tonal marks, although they are fine for solid colours and lines. The only way to achieve a tonal effect is to use mark-resist vinyl, or TruGrain, its more expensive cousin. These substrates have a smooth side and a textured side. Whatever you draw or paint on the textured side with will be held in the texture or grain, rather like drawing on Ingres paper or a lithographic plate. The grain produces a mezzotint effect. What looks tonal has actually been split up into tiny dots of solid pigment caught in the texture and therefore can be used as a very subtle positive.

These substrates love greasy media like chinagraph crayon, oil pastel and other printmaking materials such as lithographic chalks. Mark-resist can hold textural marks that look like pencil, crayon, pastel or even a watercolour-wash effect, which simply would not come out on the exposed screen if drawn on ordinary drafting film, because they would be too grey and tonal to block the light.

Black Cat by Jane Sampson – screenprint drawn on mark-resist with Indian ink.

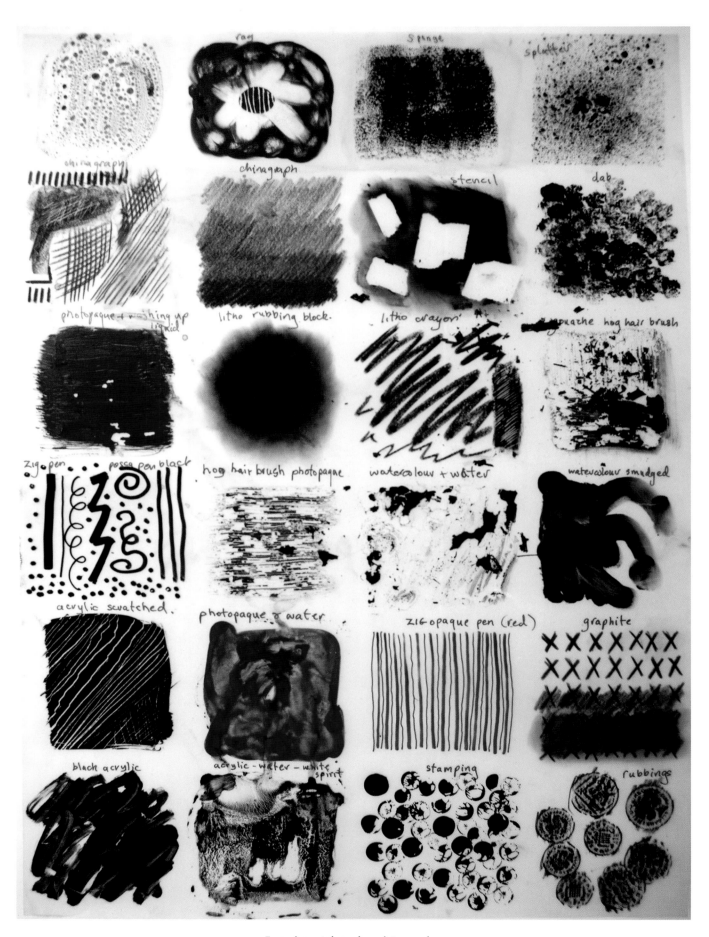

Experimental mark-resist sampler.

Close-up sequence of prints from the sampler showing different mark-making media and how they printed.

It is worth experimenting with the array of mark-making possibilities using different media on mark-resist. You can become very inventive about how you push the media around, taking advantage, for example, of the way that grease and water do not mix so as to produce organic-looking spotty effects. The results often do not look like classic screenprints at all, but more like lithographs with their subtle washes and splatters.

CHAPTER 9

HIGH-CONTRAST DIGITAL POSITIVES AND POSTERIZATIONS

Another way of using a photographic image in silkscreen is to make high-contrast separations in imitation of the high-contrast films once used in process photography. Single layers are easily achieved in Photoshop or Illustrator and can be combined in a screen-printed collage of layers with other high-contrast images in an infinite number of ways, allowing you to mix and match imagery from a wide variety of sources.

The print *Lou Lou* was constructed in Photoshop using

Lou Lou by Jane Sampson.

scanned images from old films and books as a starting point. These were digitally manipulated to make high-contrast positives, one for each colour that has been printed. The images were sized up and down, layers cut and pasted, all of the overprints conceived and planned on the computer. The layers were then printed out on a large-format inkjet printer as positives. The only thing to do after that was to play with the colours at the printing stage. Playing with colour once you have made your stencils is one of the joys of screenprinting and can transform the image.

A simple example of a way of making a high-contrast image would be to take a scan of a photograph, or to download the picture directly on to the computer from a digital camera. If the image is scanned, bear in mind how much enlargement may be involved when making the final screenprint. The standard scan is usually 300dpi, but if you are planning to blow up the image a lot, you need to compensate for possible loss of quality by scanning in at a much higher resolution, then dropping it back down after you have made the necessary enlargement, so as to avoid making huge files.

If it has come directly from a camera, the picture will be at a low resolution (usually 72dpi) but very large in physical scale, so first of all go to image size and up the resolution to the standard 300dpi, then change the size of the picture to the size you want the finished screenprint to be. For this process, you do not need the colour information, so go to:

■ Image > Mode and change it from RGB to greyscale.

There are three ways to increase the contrast in Photoshop:

■ Image > Ajustments > Brightness Contrast
■ Image > Ajustments > Levels
■ Image > Ajustments > Curves.

Any of these will work – just choose the one that seems to work best with your particular image. You are aiming to lose all of the grey tones and end up with an image that is completely black and completely white and also one that you like the look of.

This picture could, for example, be printed out on to OHP film on any inkjet printer. The printer needs to be programmed

Tree picture in greyscale.

Tree picture in RGB mode.

Tree picture rendered in high contrast.

to print on to high-quality glossy photo paper, so as to ensure that it is putting down the most black possible. This kind of OHP positive can take some time to dry, so beware of stacking up multiple positives.

Tonal separations (posterization)

A classic silkscreen technique is to make a posterized version of the original. It is a look that has become universally associated with the medium. It was originally developed as a way of manipulating photographic images and was used for making posters, hence the name. It developed when high-contrast graphic arts film, known as lith film, became commercially available. It is a method of separating a photograph into printable layers by tone. Lith film automatically reduced the tonal detail in the image to simple black and white. On film, of course, the 'white' would be transparent. A classic posterization in silkscreen would have used a large-format copy camera to photograph the original image as a negative and then either contact or project it back on to another piece of film as a positive. The resulting positive would be used to make the photostencil on a silkscreen.

By copying the same image using different exposure times, it was possible to end up with a set of images that had different amounts of detail. Those shots that were underexposed as

a negative would produce a positive with loads of black and very little detail. This layer would be screen-printed first in the lightest tone. Those that were overexposed as a negative once contacted back would produce a positive that was almost all clear film, apart from a few bits of fine detail. This layer would be screen-printed last in the darkest tone.

By making a series of these positives, an image could be separated into layers that would then be printed on top of each other in an incremental sequence going from light to dark tonally. The more layers that were made, the more 'photographic' the final image would look. It was then a question of playing with the colours to give the desired graphic effect. Later on, positive-working high-contrast films were introduced, such as Agfa Copyproof and Kodak PMT film (photo mechanical transfer), which made the whole laborious process easier and faster. In the 1960s and 1970s amongst fine artists and designers it became very popular. Think of artists such as Andy Warhol or Gert Winner.

In fact, the posterized look is now so ubiquitous that there is an automated image adjustment in Photoshop, just like all those other special photographic effects that were once achieved by dish developing in a darkroom. Unfortunately for the screen-printer, the posterize command in Photoshop gives a final result that cannot easily be split into layers and printed in an analogue fashion. However, it is perfectly possible to produce a screen-printable digital separation that mimics the multiple exposure times that would have been used on film, for example by adjusting the contrast in your image, by using levels. To those of you who like process, this is fun.

As usual with Photoshop, there are many different ways to crack the same nut. The simple step-by-step method described here, using levels, is by no means the only way of doing it.

Method

1 The original photograph that I used was a scan of a Kodachrome slide taken many years ago by my father. The original scan was made at 900dpi measuring only 3.51 × 2.37cm

1. The original scanned slide.

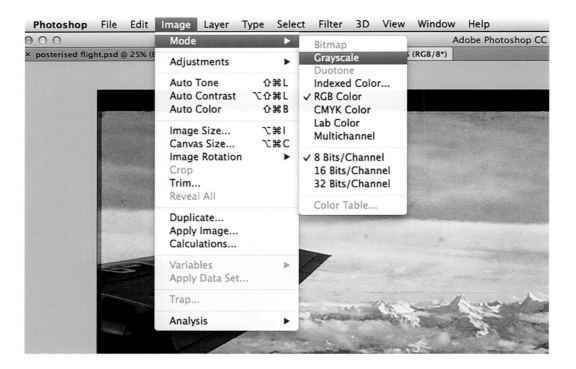

2. Change the mode to greyscale.

and saved as a high-quality jpeg. The relatively high resolution allowed me to enlarge it to roughly an A4 size (29 × 19.57cm), while dropping the resolution to the standard 300dpi without losing too much quality. Obviously the quality (the resolution) of the original image is important. A 72dpi file will not produce a satisfactory result unless you are into pixelation and artefacts.

2 Convert the image to greyscale in the mode menu.

3 Make a duplicate layer of the original in the layers palette.

2a. The image in greyscale.

3. Make a duplicate layer.

4 Working in the duplicate layer and using levels (in the Image/adjust menu), move the black and grey control sliders all the way to the right so that all three control sliders are on top of each other at the extreme right of the graph. Click 'OK' to save this layer.

5 The image should look almost completely black with a few white highlights. This is the first layer and will be printed in the

lightest colour. In fact, in practice, I decided to print a blend of colour from pale pink at the top to pale blue at the bottom to get the most subtlety out of this layer. The white highlights will stay the white of the paper throughout the printing of the image.

6 Turn off the eye icon for the new layer and click back to the original background copy in the layers palette to highlight it.

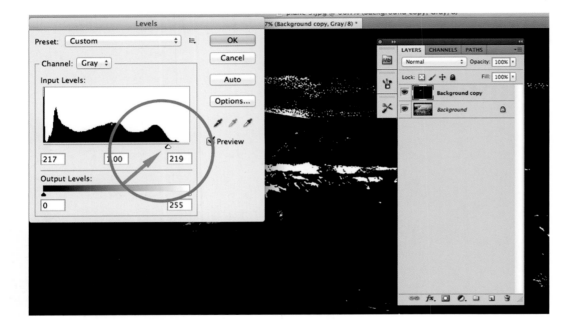

4. Move all the sliders to the right.

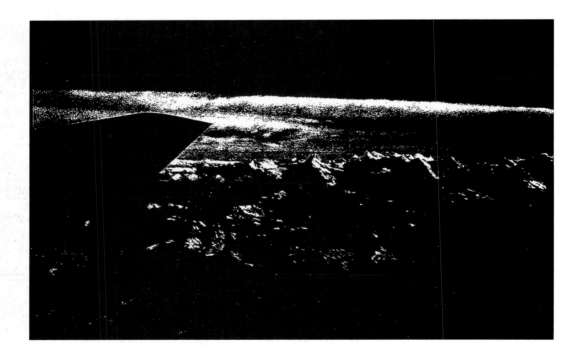

5. Layer one.

Duplicate the background layer once again and make another incremental adjustment to this second duplicate layer in levels. This time move the black and the grey control sliders to the right, but not all the way, then bring the white slider across to meet them. By bringing the sliders together, you are making

sure that the image is as high contrast as possible and that there is no grey tone in it.

7 The image should have more white highlights than the one before and will be printed in your second lightest colour.

6. Second adjusted layer.

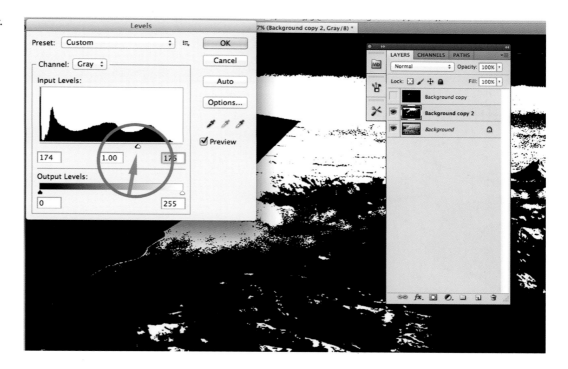

7. Second layer.

8 Continue in this way, each time making a new duplicate copy of the original background layer to work from. Slide the black and the grey sliders less to the right each time and bring the white control slider in to meet them. Save each permutation as a separate layer until you are satisfied that you have done enough, or have simply run out of room on the slider bar! The photograph of the final layer shows only the darkest areas of the image, together with the layers palette showing the sequence of layers.

9 The number of layers that you decide to use is an aesthetic decision. In this particular instance, I made seven layers so that the tonal jumps between layers were small and the final image will look almost 'photographic', rather than like a piece of graphic design. However, at the moment, all of the layers are 100 per cent opaque and it is difficult to get a sense on the computer screen of how the tonal jumps might be working. To get the feeling of what the final image might look like, I reduced the opacity of each layer to around 25 per cent.

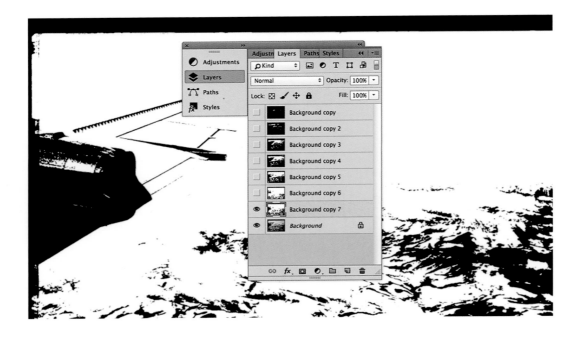

8. Making the final layer, with the layers pallet showing previous layers together with the layers palette showing the sequence of layers.

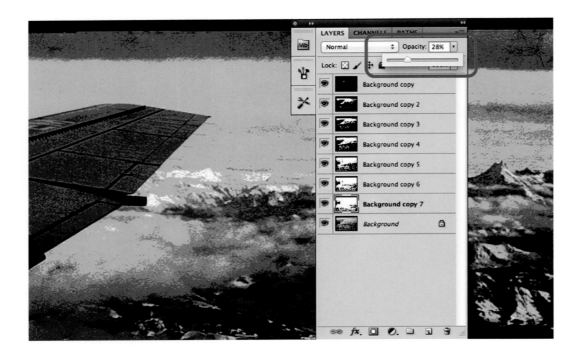

9. Changing the opacity of layers.

10 I also added a new layer, selected it all (command A) and filled it with white ('Edit' menu, then 'Fill', choosing white in the dropdown menu) and positioned it at the bottom of the stack of layers in the layers pallet (just above the background layer). This acts like putting a piece of white paper behind all the translucent layers on screen.

11 In this way, you can see how the whole image would look (although only in grey), but can also scroll up and down the layers, turning them on and off to see what they are actually doing. You may at this stage decide to add or delete a layer, for example.

10. Making a new white layer.

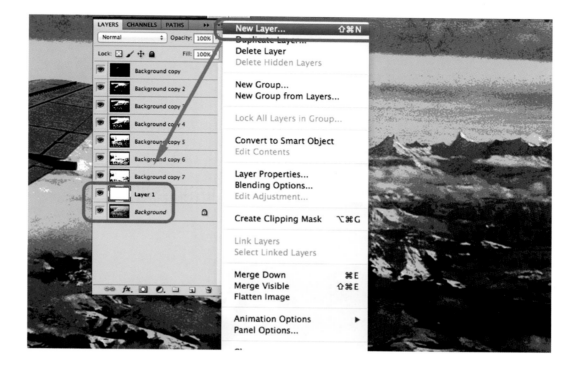

11. Final layered image.

12 When you are happy with all of the layers, it is time to make them all 100 per cent opaque again and print them out on to film, one by one, ready to expose on to the screen. It is a good idea to add registration marks to the printout. This can usually be done by the printer driver at the print stage.

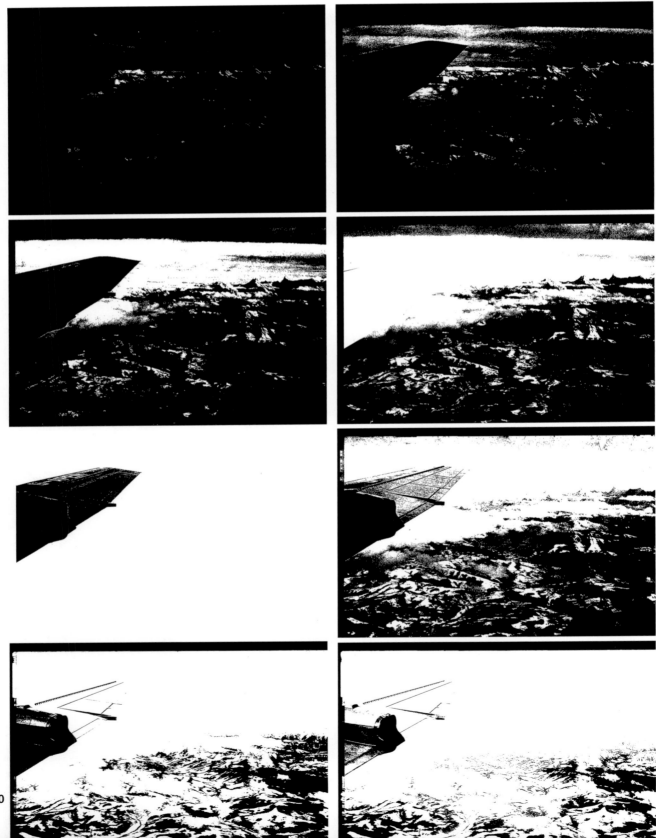

12. PREVIOUS PAGE AND BELOW: **Corresponding sequence of colour layers printed.**

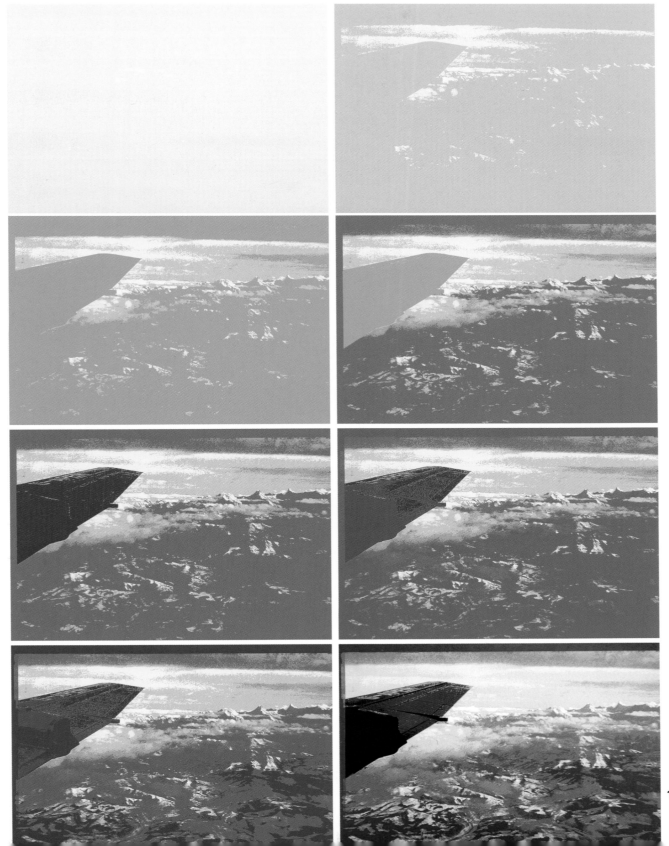

Posterizations do not have to be as detailed as this photographic-looking example. More graphic or decorative effects can be achieved in three or four colours, using one of the more detailed separations on top of blocks of colour.

Final printed silkscreen.

CHAPTER 10

DEALING WITH HALFTONES AND BITMAPS

I have been teaching silkscreenprinting classes for many years and in almost every class there will be one or more students who want to use a photograph in a project. At first this seems quite easy, but it is actually not that simple. It is possible to achieve a good result just by following a few simple steps, but it is useful to explain some of the theory behind the techniques. If you are itching to get stuff on screen and start printing, feel free to skip the theory. If you want to know why you need to do certain things, the limitations of the process and how to achieve the results that you have in your mind's eye, then I would urge you to read this next bit to become familiar with the theory.

The theory

A black and white photograph has only a single colour – black. There are also greys, but these are just black that has been diluted by various degrees. The white areas are just where there is no black at all. We call this kind of image a greyscale image. If the colour is one that is other than black, we call it a monochrome image, but it is still greyscale if it contains dilutions of the same base colour. When screen-printing such an image, we have two problems.

Firstly, when we make a stencil, the black areas of our positive result in open areas of mesh where the ink can pass through and print, whereas the transparent areas result in the emulsion being exposed and hardening to form the stencil itself, which blocks the mesh in those places so that they do not print. If there is grey in the positive, whether enough light passes through to expose the emulsion will depend upon the shade of grey. There will be a critical value of grey at which it will block the light and that area will print. Any lighter and the emulsion will be exposed and those areas will become stencil.

Secondly, we have a similar problem with the ink. Ours is black, so how do we print grey with it? If you were painting, you could dilute each brush load by the appropriate amount and blend it in with surrounding areas of paint. However, you cannot do this when you are screen-printing. All is not lost, however, as we can simulate greys using an optical illusion, namely dots, which in print-speak are called halftones.

Most printing techniques, with the exception of photogravure and sublimation printing, use the halftone to produce the illusion of shades of grey and of colour. There are two types of halftone: the conventional one, in which the shade depends upon the size of dot, and the diffusion dither, or stochastic halftone, where all the dots are the same size and the illusion of different shades depends upon the number of dots in a certain area.

Conventional or mechanical halftone

In this type of halftone, the dots are laid out along straight lines and the angle that these lines of dots make against a line

Conventional halftone.

Low- and high-frequency
halftones.

running horizontally through the document is called the screen angle. The dots have a frequency, usually measured in lines per inch (lpi), or per centimetre. A high-frequency halftone has a lot of dots in a unit length, so the dots are small. A low-frequency halftone has fewer, bigger dots, so a low lpi. The look of this type of halftone is smooth, mechanical and regular and it is often associated with screenprints, especially if the dots are large enough to be clearly visible from a distance.

In theory, the finer the dot, the more detailed and realistic the result, but unfortunately this is not the case with screenprints. There is a limit as to how small a dot can be screened, meaning that very light greys (very small dots) will not print. At the other end, very large dots will tend to flood, so very dark greys will print as black. These effects increase as the dot frequency increases and the dots get smaller. If you want your print to look good, working by hand rather than on an automated machine, you will need to have a fairly low-frequency/big-dot halftone on your artwork. For example, 64lpi is really the maximum line count that you would want to use; 54lpi and 45lpi will still look good, but be much easier to print properly.

The angle of the halftone can be important to avoid moiré, the strange effect produced when two regular patterns are superimposed, in this case the threads of the fabric and the dots of the halftone. The nicest-looking angle for the dots is 45 degrees, although this may be prone to moiré; 25 degrees almost guarantees a moiré-free stencil, but it does not look quite as good.

This type of halftone is very even looking – the dots can be aesthetically pleasing and become a feature in their own right. However, because this halftone is so smooth, problems can stick out like a sore thumb.

Diffusion dither/stochastic halftone

This type of halftone is how an inkjet printer produces shades of colour. The dots are all the same size, but the number of them in a given area determines the shade that is perceived. It can look a bit untidy, especially if the dots are quite big. As with a conventional halftone, if the dots are too small there will

Stochastic dots.

Low stochastic dot count.

be problems printing them as a screenprint. On a 90T mesh, a frequency of 160lpi is good – any higher and they will dry in quickly; any lower and the dots tend to join up and form worm-like shapes that can look odd.

The practice

You can convert your image to halftone in image editing software such as Photoshop, or if you have a laser printer and page layout software such as Illustrator or InDesign, you can add a conventional halftone when printing out your positive. The latter is much more straightforward, but you can only print out a conventional halftone, and not a diffusion dither, if you let the RIP do the halftoning.

Using Photoshop

Open your image file and go to:

- 'Image' > 'Mode' > 'Greyscale'
- In Photoshop, you will see the discard colour information dialogue box: select 'Discard'. If you decide that it is not quite the result that you want, cancel and take them up on their suggestion:
- 'Image' > 'Adjustments' > 'Black & White'
- This gives you much greater control over the balance of greys in the converted file.

- Once your file has been converted:
- 'Save As' > 'filename grey'.

In order to get a nice-looking halftone you will need a resolution of at least 300dpi at the size that you want to print. Go to:

- 'Image' > 'Image Size'
- In the dialogue box, make sure that the 'Constrain Proportions' box is ticked. Having made sure that the size that you want your image to print will fit on both your paper and screen, change the larger dimension to the size required. The shorter dimension will change automatically
- Enter a resolution that is 300dpi minimum. The higher the resolution, the better, but keep your eye on the image size, keeping it to a figure that your computer can handle without too much strain. Go to:
- 'Image' > 'Mode' > 'Bitmap'
- A pop-up box will ask you to flatten the image, click 'Yes'. Here you can choose to render your image as either a conventional halftone or a diffusion dither. To render it as a conventional halftone, 'Output' should be set to something like 600dpi. The higher this figure, the smoother the dot will be. Go to:
- 'Method' > 'Halftone Screen'
- You will now see the halftone dialogue box and here you decide how ambitious you are going to be. If you are using a 90T mesh, frequencies of 45 or 55lpi are probably the best choices. You could try higher frequencies like 65lpi, but any more and the result is

Examples of different halftones, 'Diamond' and 'Lines'.

unlikely to look good. Using a 90T mesh, 45, 55 and 65lpi are the line counts that are the least likely to produce interference patterns. After you have chosen a suitable frequency, you need to select an angle. As previously stated, 45 degrees looks best; however, 25 degrees will give the fewest problems with screen clash

■ Now you need to select the shape of the dot. In the dropdown menu there will be a list of possible dot shapes:
■ 'Round' (recommended for light images such as skin tones)
■ 'Diamond'
■ 'Ellipse' (recommended when there are lots of objects)
■ 'Line'
■ 'Square' (recommended for images with lots of detail)
■ 'Cross'.

Note that 'Line' produces a halftone which is not strictly dots, but it works in the same way and there are plug-ins that enable the halftone output to be in circular lines like old engravings. It is probably a good idea to try the different dot shapes so that you can choose the one you prefer, but they will need to be printed on to paper to see what they are really like, because bitmaps can look awful on the computer display owing to moiré effects.

You can either save the resulting different bitmaps, or print out each shape and then 'Revert' to the greyscale stage, but it is best to keep the greyscale document intact, so if you do save any of the bitmaps, use the 'Save As ...' command. Once you

have decided on the dot frequency, shape and angle, you can print out the bitmap. It is always a good idea to print out on to paper first just to make sure all is well. Use the same settings as you would for your final printout on to film. You may experience moiré patterns in the printout. This generally tends to happen if the halftone is too fine and can usually be sorted out by slightly changing the halftone frequency or angle.

Output using page layout software and laser printer

A laser printer uses halftones to print greys, so it has built-in software (RIP) that converts greyscale to halftone. This halftone is usually too fine to use in screenprinting, but the settings can be customized to an output that can be used.

Firstly, convert your image to greyscale and make sure that the image resolution is at least 300dpi at the size you wish to print it (*see* previous section). Now create a new document in the page layout software – make sure that the document size matches the size of your print medium. Place your greyscale file in the document, make any size adjustments you feel necessary, add text, register marks and crop marks if required, then go to 'Print'.

Somewhere in the box there will be a menu item called 'Output'. Click on this and you should see a section appear in the dialogue box also labelled 'Output'. The dropdown menu 'Mode' will be set to 'Composite'. Change to 'Separations (Host-Based)'. In the 'Document Ink Options' make sure that

Circular line screen.

Example of a print dialogue box. (NB: your print dialogue box may not look identical to this one.)

only the 'Process Black' line is active (usually indicated by a tick or cute little picture of a printer).

There are three columns: 'Frequency'; 'Angle'; 'Dot Shape'. Once you have chosen these three parameters, press 'Print' and see what the result is. Don't forget that it is always a good idea to print out on paper first just to make sure that all is well. If it looks good, print out your film.

There is, of course, another option – you can send the file to a professional typesetter to run a positive for you. This can be expensive and you must specify *exactly* what you want in terms of all the parameters. The film you get back will be superb quality, but there is the chance that it may not be quite what you were expecting, so it is probably best not to use a professional typesetter until you have reached a good level of competency. The best quality is the traditional silver film. Inkjet films can be okay, but quite often they can be a bit 'thin', so if you are a fan of thick stencils requiring longer exposure times, use silver.

One of the biggest advantages of getting your films run out at a typesetting bureau is that they can usually run far larger films than you can at home – if you have ever tried tiling small films together to make a large halftone positive you will know that the joins always show!

Making a halftone screen

Making a screen from your halftone film will require good technique. Inspect your film closely. If it is a conventional halftone you will see that the light grey areas have tiny dots and the dark grey areas have tiny holes in great swathes of black. Getting the optimum exposure time is vital – too long an exposure and all the tiny dots will burn through; too short an exposure and the tiny bits of stencil in the dark areas may not come out and, in the worst case scenario, the fine detail will just wash out when you develop the stencil. If your halftone is a diffusion dither, *all* the dots are going to be small, but you are still going to have parts where the area between those dots needs to be correctly exposed, or it will just print as a solid black (or whatever colour you are using).

In addition, there is moiré to contend with. You can deal with this in the following way. Before coating your screen, place it over a lightbox, or on a table, print side uppermost with a white sheet of paper underneath. Place your positive on the screen as you would for an exposure, with the emulsion side against the mesh, and see if there are any unwanted patterns. Surprisingly, you may not spot them straightaway, but if you rotate the positive they may suddenly jump out at you.

Rotate the positive until the patterns are at their least noticeable and make a note of the angle it makes with the frame. A good way of doing this is to lay a sheet of paper with one edge butting up to the positive, then make two marks where the paper meets the frame. When you have coated and dried the screen, use the piece of paper to position the positive, tape it in place so that it does not move and do your exposure.

In order to expose your halftone correctly, you will need to know the best exposure time for fine detail (*see* the exposure calculator in Chapter 7). It is important that your positive is in contact with the surface of the emulsion – any gaps between the two will allow the light to spread under the image, turning small dots into no dots. Dust, hairs, warped frames and kinks in the film can all prevent the positive from having good contact with the screen. If you are exposing through glass and there are scratches in the image area, these will show in the finished stencil. A way of avoiding this is to split the exposure into two or even three parts, moving the screen between each part-exposure. The separate exposures should add up to the time you have worked out using the exposure calculator and it is vital that the positive is taped (with see-through tape) to the screen, so that it cannot move during the process.

When developing the screen, be thorough with the washing out, but try not to use too much force. Over-zealous spraying can wash away the fine detail. When you have washed out the image, remove as much water as possible from the open mesh. A good-quality chamois leather is ideal for this, using a gentle dabbing motion on the print side (the chamois should be damp, but not wet). Dry the screen flat. If it is dried vertically, invariably there will be drops of water trapped where the mesh meets the frame and these will run down the stencil and possibly leave traces of chemical in the open areas.

Now we finally come to the difficult part – the printing. Halftone prints are very unforgiving. Small particles of dust or grit,

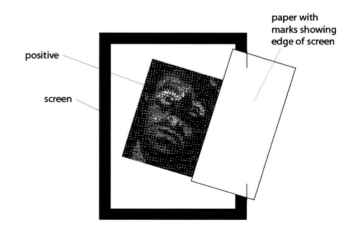

Rotate the positive on the screen and mark using a sheet of paper.

on or under the paper, are immediately obvious. Small problems quickly escalate into big ones. The smaller dots tend to dry in, while the darker areas tend to flood, leading to zones in the print.

Sounds bad, doesn't it? However, with good preparation the process can be straightforward. You will give yourself the best chance by following this list as much as possible:

- A good, well-stretched screen with plenty of room for the image.
- A good squeegee with a straight, sharp edge, preferably medium bladed – brand new is ideal. Remember that there needs to be good overlap at each side of the print and if you have rotated the positive to eliminate moiré, a bigger squeegee than anticipated might be needed.
- A good supply of well-mixed ink with a slightly stiffer consistency than normal. Some inks are specifically formulated for halftone printing, with a gel structure to help keep a clean dot. Often these inks are thixotropic, which means that when they are subjected to a force they will readily flow, but when the force is no longer there, they become stiff (a mixture of cornflour paste in water has this property). When you do your print stroke, the ink will flow through the mesh, but once it hits the paper, it will stay put. The downside of this type of ink is that it can creep up the squeegee blade, leaving too little on the screen surface – the remedy is to use plenty and be prepared to scrape the ink regularly back on to the screen surface with something like an old credit card.
- Plenty of clean, uncoated paper with a reasonably absorbent surface for printing out. A smooth paper with a tight surface for your actual edition.
- A good supply of water and clean cloths (plain T-shirts are hard to beat) cut to convenient sizes.
- Somewhere to put your precious prints when they have been printed.
- An optional extra is someone to give you a helping hand.

Important printing points

In theory, halftone printing is no more difficult than printing line artwork. However, it does have its own problems and needs a slightly different technique. Good squeegee technique is essential. The most common fault with beginners is pushing too much ink through the mesh, resulting in fine detail being submerged in large quantities of ink and a very dark, messy print.

This is known as flooding. There can be several possible causes:

- the squeegee angle being too shallow on flood stroke, print stroke, or both
- too much force being applied to the squeegee, bending the blade
- the mesh being charged with too much ink from an over-enthusiastic flood
- multiple floods or print strokes.

It is important to realize that the squeegee does not 'shove' the ink through the mesh – the purpose of the flood stroke is to fill the holes in the mesh with ink and the print stroke presses the stencil down so that it touches the paper along the length of the squeegee. The weight of the ink carried in front of the blade, combined with the 'stickiness' of the paper, is what causes the ink to leave the stencil and be deposited on the paper. When printing halftones, both the flood and print strokes should be at a steeper angle than normal, to avoid forcing too much ink through the stencil. Consequently, the effort needed is perhaps more than is usually required with line artwork.

It is important to have a good snap-off – the amount will depend upon the tension of the screen, the consistency of the ink and your strength. It should feel like slightly hard work, but not shoulder-popping effort.

When you begin the run, print out a few copies on *clean* practice paper. Start with a flood angle of about 40 degrees to the vertical and your print stroke about 20 degrees. Increase your squeegee angle with each successive print (not the flood), until you get a good-looking print with a reasonable amount of pressure. Do not flood more than once – just make sure that you always have enough ink to get a successful flood.

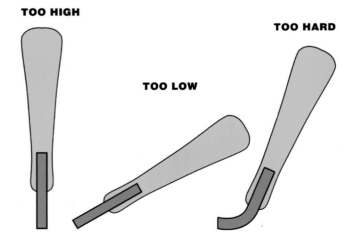

TOO HIGH

TOO HARD

TOO LOW

Diagram of squeegee angles.

DIRECTION OF PRINT

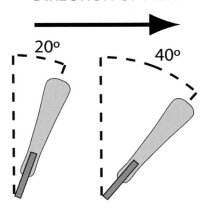

Diagram of squeegee angle.

Do not print more than once.

When you feel you have a decent print, do one on your good paper and quickly compare it to the positive, looking for areas that have dried in, or ones that have flooded. The first print will most likely be the best one. Put it somewhere you can see it and compare each subsequent print to that one, trying to keep the quality the same – in the heat of the print run it is easy to miss things going wrong, as there are so many things to attend to, but don't spend too long on this. You need to work quickly, but calmly. Aim to be making one print every 30sec or so. If the quality starts to go, stop printing on your good paper, work out what's going wrong, and fix it – don't just carry on regardless.

When you have fixed a problem, always restart your run in the same way – make sure you have a good quantity of ink in front of your squeegee and print, without flooding, on to a clean, flat, dry piece of paper. Keep doing this on fresh paper until the print is free from smudges and defects. Flood and resume your printing run properly.

Other problems

If light areas are not printing, in all probability the ink has dried in the smaller dots. This can be due to:

- insufficient pressure on your print stroke
- ink too thick
- your chosen paper has a surface coating that is being absorbed by the ink in the mesh
- not printing fast enough.

Pick-up Truck by Jodie Tableporter. The bitmapped image of the pick-up truck (using diffusion dither) has been printed in translucent purple over solid blocks of colour (blue and yellow). The stencils for the blue and yellow layers were hand-cut from red masking film and exposed on to the screen.

CHAPTER 11

FOUR-COLOUR SEPARATIONS

In the previous chapter, we covered how it is possible to screen-print a black and white photograph using halftones. We do not have to stop there. We can screen-print full-colour images as well. It is probably worth saying here that if you want to make copies of a colour photo or scan, there are better ways of doing it, but once you have nailed the techniques used in halftone printing, printing in full colour can be great fun and the limitations of the screen-print process mean that although the final result will not be an exact reproduction of the original, you will end up with a unique print with an attractive, distinctive look.

If you're so eager to print in full colour that you've skipped the section on printing halftones, please go back and read it, because you will need to know everything covered in that chapter. Also, it is a good idea to warm up on a few simple greyscale prints before you leap into full colour. If you want to read a brief rundown on colour theory as it relates to printing, *see* Chapter 12. If you just want to get stuck in, this chapter will give you the 'how to'.

Firstly, it is possible to make a full colour print by using just four colours:

- cyan
- magenta
- yellow
- black.

These colours are collectively known as CMYK. A coloured image can be separated into these four colours. Each of these separations is a monochrome greyscale image that can be converted to halftones and exposed on screen. If these stencils are printed in the appropriate colour, when they are all printed in register they give the illusion of a picture in full colour.

BELOW: **Halftone colour separation building up.**

OPPOSITE PAGE: **Finished print with black added.** *You don't forget, you just move on* **by Jack Nash.**

cyan

cyan and magenta

cyan, magenta and yellow

Screenprint made using four dithered (stochastic) separations. *It's easier to think that you are in love than it is to accept that you are alone* by Jack Nash. NB: the sky was added as a spot colour.

Using image-editing software

As with a monochrome halftone, film positives can be produced using image-editing software or page layout software. As most digital images are in RGB colour mode, the first step is to convert your image to CMYK. Go to:

■   'Image' > 'Mode' > 'CMYK colour'.

If you make the Channels window visible, you should see five layers – the topmost is called 'CMYK'; the rest are each named after one of the trichromatic colours. Next, using the image menu, make sure that the 'Constrain Proportions' box is ticked and alter the image size to what you want the print to be. Change the resolution to something above 300dpi. Make this as high as possible without it being too much for your computer to handle without strain.

Now bring up the Channels window. In the drop-down menu accessed through that window there is an instruction, 'Split Channels'. When Photoshop has done its work, the full-colour picture you had on screen previously will have been replaced by a stack of four greyscale images, all the same size and resolution. These are your picture split into its colour separations. Save these one by one.

Finally, you need to convert these greyscale images to halftones or diffusion dither. Diffusion dither prints sometimes look a bit scruffy, but they avoid moiré.

Using diffusion dither

Should you decide to use dithered separations, follow these instructions:

■   'Image' > 'Mode' > 'Bitmap'.

In the Bitmap box, set 'Output' to 160 pixels per inch, set 'Use' to 'Diffusion Dither'.

NB: the figure 160 assumes that you are using a 90T screen; with a finer screen you could go for a slightly higher count, or with a coarser screen you would need to go lower. Save your bitmap and do the same with the remaining colours, keeping the Bitmap settings the same. Print them out and get cracking.

Detail showing the dot structure.

Using conventional halftone

If you opt to use a conventional halftone, you will need to decide on the frequency and shape of the dots. Go to:

■ 'Image' > 'Mode' > 'Bitmap'.

This time, your output should be as high as you dare make it and the method is 'Halftone'. In the 'Halftone Screen' box, set the frequency to either 45, 54 or 65 lines per inch. If you are using a 90 mesh, these frequencies are reputed to have minimal moiré. 45lpi may sound coarse, but the dots are not prominent and it will be far easier to print than the higher line counts.

Previously, when you have printed conventional halftones, you will have almost certainly come across moiré when exposing your screen. To refresh your memory, these are patterns produced when two regular patterns are superimposed – in this case, the screen mesh and the halftone dots.

You are about to make a print that features not just two, but four regular patterns (if you don't count the screen mesh) and if you thought that the potential for moiré was greatly increased, you would be right. There is no need to be unduly concerned though, as choosing the correct angle for each of the different halftones can almost eliminate the problem. There are many recipes for setting up the angles for each of the colours, but the most common one is:

■ C = 15 degrees, M = 45 degrees, Y = 0 degrees, and K (black) = 75 degrees.

I would recommend that you convert just one of the colours into a halftone to start with (preferably the one with the biggest range of mid-grey), print that out on to film and check it for moiré on the uncoated screen you intend to use. It may be that it is impossible to make the patterns unnoticeable no matter how much you turn the positive on the screen. In this case, redo the conversion to bitmap, but alter the frequency by a couple of lines per inch and have another go. When you have found a line count that is satisfactory, go ahead and convert the colour separations into halftones, keeping all the settings the same for each colour, apart from the angles that you can specify as above. Save these files, but keep the greyscale files intact, just in case you decide to change something at a later stage.

I find it useful to put the line count in the bitmap file title, since once the file has been converted there is no way of finding out the dot frequency, short of actually counting how many there are in a given distance.

Using page layout software

This is the easiest way (short of getting the films run out at a bureau) to get a full set of positives. Remember that you have to have a printer with a postscript RIP for this to work.

Simply open a new document, place your image in the document, resize it if necessary, add any registration marks, extra text and so on, then save the document. The image can be either CMYK or RBG. Go to print the document.

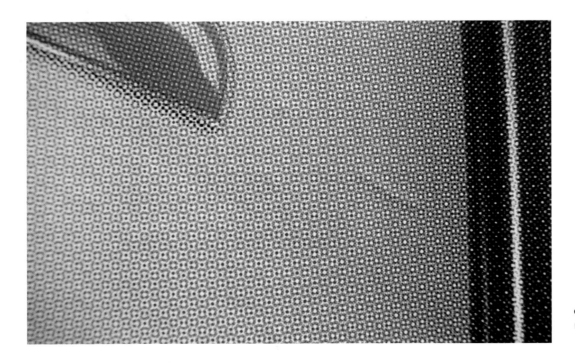

Detail of a halftone separation showing the typical 'rosette' pattern created when the layers are registered correctly and the screen angles are correct.

Enlarged section of an artfully misregistered halftone, done for the 'effect'.

Click on the line/button labelled 'Output' and the 'Print' dialogue box will change to something similar to the version shown here.

Change Mode to 'Separations (Host-Based)', then in the list of 'Document Ink Options' enter your chosen values for 'Frequency', 'Angle' and 'Dot Shape'. If you were to press 'Print' now, all four separations would print out. After years of experiencing unexpected things happening at the printout stage, I personally would choose to print the separations one at a time. The way this is done is to click on the little printer icons until just one is left – this is the one that will print out. When it is finished, check the result and if all is well, turn off the colour that has just printed, make another colour active and print it out. Repeat until you have the complete set of four.

All that remains is to put the images on screen and print the separations. Most of the information about screen making and printing has already been covered in Chapter 10 halftones – after all, a full-colour print is just four halftones layered in the same image. A few additional things need to be mentioned, however.

The ideal scenario would be that the four separations are put up on four separate screens, all the same size, mesh count and tension. If all the colours are put on to the same screen, they will almost certainly be too close to the frame to print properly.

Print dialogue box.

This will lead to a much greater chance that the printing ink will become contaminated by traces from previous colours, plus if anything catastrophic should happen to the screen, you will have lost all the colours not yet printed. If the colours are on their own screens, there will be plenty of space to angle the positive if necessary, and there is no chance that the colour you are printing will be contaminated by previous ones. Four screens would be a large investment, but two screens with two colours on each is also worth thinking about. I understand that some people have a large screen and do not really have a choice, but the closer your image is to the frame or another colour that has been masked off, the more likely it is to mess up. If you are trying to make a good print, you should consider space around your image as a necessity, rather than a luxury.

Printing order

Traditionally, the yellow is the first colour printed, but it is really difficult to see if it is printing all right. I have tried wearing 3D glasses (modified so that they had two purple lenses) whilst printing the yellow. It works. You can see the yellow really clearly, but it is not a pleasant experience. In reality, it makes very little noticeable difference whatever order the colours are printed in. So, for a beginner, it is probably best to start with the cyan, then yellow, then magenta. It is important that the black should be printed last. NB: Allow plenty of time for your prints to dry between colours, but do not be tempted to force-dry them. By all means put a hairdryer or fan on them, but absolutely no heat, because warm air will cause the paper to change shape and then your colours will not fit.

CHAPTER 12

COLOUR THEORY

I mentioned in the previous chapter that it is possible to produce a screenprint in full colour without really needing to know how the process works. However, I am sure there will be plenty of readers who want to know more about the theory, so I will attempt to explain. Seeing in colour is a mysterious process and we still do not fully understand how it works, but it is possible to explain it with a greatly simplified model that is approximately correct (a bit like the Relativistic versus the Newtonian view of the Universe!).

Firstly, the eye has three types of colour receptors, which are sensitive to red, green or blue. If you examine a computer monitor screen through a magnifying glass, you will see that it is made up of tiny dots of these colours. Practically all the colours in the material world can be reproduced on a TV screen using these three colours in varying proportions (although a TV screen will have a bit of trouble with fluorescents and metallics – they look good until you compare them to the real thing).

So in order to screen-print in full colour, all we need to do is to separate the image into the three colours (usually abbreviated to RGB) that are known as the primary colours and print them. Right? Well, no. Unfortunately it does not work like that, because the only way we can actually see something is if light is coming from the object and reaches our eyes. The light is either made by the object itself, or is coming from another source and is reflected by the object – transmitted versus reflected light.

Transmitted light comes from the sun, TV screens, stars, house lights, street lights and so on. If a light source appears red, that is because the light it is emitting is predominantly red. If it appears yellow, it is because the source is emitting green and red light, and our brain interprets this mixture as yellow:

- red + green = yellow.

It is almost certain that you have spent a sizeable portion of your life mixing paints to get the right colour, both at school and, as you are interested in screenprinting, afterwards. If the assertion that red + green = yellow starts to ring a few alarm bells, this is quite understandable. When I was a child, if you mixed red and green paint, you got brown. This is still true and

it works with Plasticine as well. This is because we see most of the objects around us because they reflect light.

For all intents and purposes, daylight can be considered white – a mixture of red, blue and green light. (It also contains lots of other colours, like infra-red, ultraviolet, X-rays and so on, but they are not really relevant here because we can't see them.) When you see an object in daylight and it appears red, this is because the object has absorbed the green and blue portions of the light and all that gets reflected to your eye is the red. If you see an object and it appears green, this is because it has absorbed the red and blue components of the white light, reflecting only the green. When I use the term 'object', this includes things like paint and ink.

If you mix a green ink and a red ink, you will have a mixture that will absorb red and blue (from the green) and green and blue (from the red). The colour of the mixture is the colour that is reflected after all the absorption has taken place. When you mix red and green ink, the colours that are absorbed are red, green and blue. Basically, all of the colours have been absorbed. In theory, that means that the mixture should be black, but it is not a perfect world, so the colour you get is a sort of brown/grey, the exact shade depending upon how strong each of the colours is.

So, now we know that mixing light colours and mixing ink colours give completely different results. Mix red, green and blue light together and you get white. Mix red, green and blue inks together and you get sludge. Also, note that:

- no light = black
- no ink = white (as long as you are printing on white paper).

As previously stated, with regard to light sources, just red, green and blue are needed to produce all the colours that we see. For this reason, these particular colours are referred to as the primary colours and because you can make different colours by adding them together, they are known as the *additive primaries* (although *light primaries* might be easier to remember).

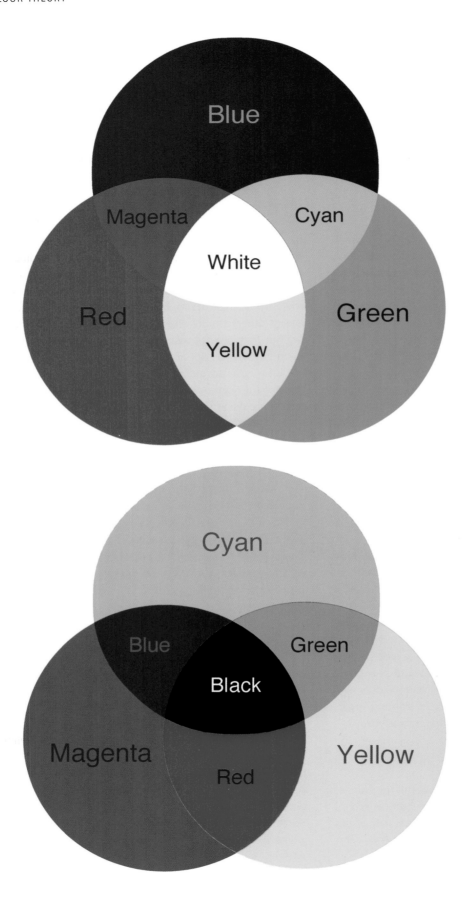

The three primaries – red, blue and green – and their secondary colours – cyan, magenta and yellow – together with white.

The three secondaries, or process colours, and the colours they make when overprinted.

When referring to ink colours, there is also a set of colours from which all the other colours can be made. These colours are cyan, magenta and yellow. In theory, if we mix all three we should get black, but this is seldom the case in practice. The overprint areas that should be black are more often a dark muddy colour, so a black was added to the set of colours to overcome this problem. These four colours are collectively known as CMYK, the full colour set, or the four-colour set. This set of colours is also a primary set, but they are known as *subtractive primaries*:

- they are *primaries* because they can be used to make most other colours
- they are *subtractive* because they subtract colours from white and the colour you see is the one that remains. Think of them as *print primaries*.

The relationship between the two sets of primaries is quite simple. When two additive primaries are combined, you get a secondary. That secondary is a subtractive (print) primary:

- blue + green = cyan
- red + green = yellow
- blue + red = magenta.

The diagrams reprinted here show that when using both systems, either light primaries or print primaries, pretty much the same range of colours can be achieved, or at least close enough to look okay. The truth is that a print made using the print primaries can look good, but it is just not capable of representing the colour range of an LCD screen, while a screen will never be able to capture what is out there in the real world. The range of colours that can be represented is called the Gamut. Expanding the range of colour by using a system of six colours has been explored. It is basically the CMYK set with the addition of an orange and a green, colours that do not come out too well in four-colour prints. This system is called Hexamatic printing, or Hex for short, but it does not seem to have caught on.

Hopefully, you understand a bit about colour theory now. It probably won't make a lot of difference to your prints, but it is one of those things that every printer should know!

GLOSSARY

A

Acid-free paper

Paper that if infused in water will have a neutral pH (7 or slightly greater). Unlike paper made from wood pulp, like newsprint, for example, it does not yellow with age, become brittle, or react with the inks printed on it over time, therefore preserving the artwork for longer.

Amberlith (or Rubylith)

Brand names of light-safe knife-cut masking films that are coated on to a clear polyester backing sheet. Being light-safe, they block the ultraviolet light of an exposure unit and are therefore used to make positives either by hand or on a digital plotter.

APF

Stands for assigned protection factor when referring to face masks and respirators.

B

Bitmap

An image file on a computer used to store digital images (literally a map of bits). Halftones and dithers used to simulate tone in screenprintng are known as bitmaps. Image editing software like Photoshop uses bitmap.

Bleed

Sometimes also called trapping. It is when the areas of colour in one colour layer of a print are deliberately made very slightly larger than necessary so that the next layer of colour will slightly overlap them, thus preventing telltale white lines around tightly registered layers.

Bleeding

When the printed ink spreads outside of its printed area and 'bleeds' into the surrounding paper. The causes of this are usually either too much snap-off, a stencil that is underexposed and therefore too thin, or ink that is too thin. Sometimes it is a combination of all of these things.

Butt registration

When two printed colours meet edge to edge without overlapping.

C

Capillary film

Pre-sensitized emulsion coated on a polyester base, usually supplied by the roll and cut to size. There are many different types for different print applications. The film is exposed and then applied to the damp screen by capillary action, hence the name. Once dried, the backing sheet is peeled off, leaving a stencil that is very accurate and of uniform thickness. This is its main advantage over direct stencils.

Coating trough

Sometimes also called a scoop coater. This is the implement used to apply a direct photoemulsion in an even layer on to a screen.

Cockling

With reference to printing, this is where the printed paper wrinkles in areas of high ink coverage and is no longer flat. The paper fibre deforms and swells. Solutions to this are to use a heavier weight of paper, or a finer screen that does not lay down so much ink.

Continuous tone

The tones in a photographic image ranging from black to white in a (theoretically) infinite range of greys. It generally describes a traditional photograph produced photo-chemically, rather than a digital or printed version.

COSHH Assessment

This refers to risk-assessment guidelines to assess and control hazards in the workplace. Such guidelines are readily available online and are essential to carry out if you are going to work with members of the public, or employ anyone to work for you, in order to ensure compliance with health and safety laws.

D

Deckle edge

The deckle is a wooden frame used in handmade paper-making. It is put into the paper mould to prevent the paper pulp from spreading beyond its bounds, thus controlling the size of the sheet when the mould is dipped into the vat of pulp. The slurry of pulp seeps under the deckle to produce the characteristic feathered edge. This has become a traditional status symbol in printmaking and book arts circles and even though most papers are not produced this way anymore, the deckled edge is still a feature of high-quality printmaking papers.

Diffusion dither

Used to create the illusion of continuous tone (like a photograph) in the final printed result, the diffusion dither option in Photoshop (in the bitmap menu) generates a pseudo-random pattern of dots that is usually less noticeable than the classic halftone. Unlike the classic halftone, where the dots are of differing sizes, and in a regular pattern, all of the dots in a diffusion dither are the same size but are spaced closer or further apart. There will be more dots where the image is darker and fewer dots where it is lighter. Images treated in this way often have a soft grainy look.

Direct stencil

When sensitized liquid photoemulsion is applied to the screen mesh with a coating trough, dried and then exposed, the stencil is known as a direct stencil.

Durometer

A Durometer is a device developed by Alfred F. Shore in the 1920s to measure the relative hardness of a material. It is often used to measure the hardness of materials like polymers and rubbers. He also defined the durometer scale of measurement. The hardness or softness of squeegee blades is measured in durometers.

Dynamic screens

Retensionable screen frames that can stretch the mesh when they are recovered and can be tightened up during the life of the screen, giving greater accuracy in registration for longer. They are often roller frames that use opposing roller bars to stretch the mesh and the roller forms the frame.

E

Edition

An edition of prints is a set of prints that are all the same. Editions are either unlimited or limited. A limited edition is numbered and signed (1/20, 2/20 and so on). It guarantees to the collector that no more of the same print will be printed once the edition is sold out, thus making the limited-edition print more valuable than one that is unlimited.

Exposure latitude

The range of exposure time that will produce a usable stencil when exposing a screen.

Extender base

Another name for screen-printing medium or reducing medium, which, when added to acrylic paint or screen-printing ink, will increase transparency and volume, and will smooth the texture to give the right consistency. It often contains a retardant to slow down the drying time of the mixture, thus preventing the ink from drying in the mesh while printing.

F

Filler

Sometimes called screen block. This can be painted or scraped thinly on to the screen to block large areas, define printing areas, or spot out dust spots and pinholes if they occur in photographic stencils. There are different types: some resist water for use with water-based inks; some resist solvent for use with solvent-based inks; and some resist both solvent and water.

Flood and stroke

When printing, the flood stroke is when the mesh is filled with ink ready for the print stroke and the ink is forced through the mesh using the squeegee.

Four-colour separation

In commercial printing, the four-colour process uses the four process colours – cyan, magenta, yellow and black (CMYK) – as a method of reproducing a full-colour image, usually a photograph. Each colour layer is split into a system of dots (halftones), which, when printed together (in sequence and in register), give the illusion that you are looking at a full-colour image.

G

Ghosting

When an old image mysteriously starts reappearing during the printing of a new stencil it is called ghosting. This means that the screen needs a more thorough cleansing than just removing the stencil when recycling and will involve using a caustic-based cleaning paste to remove all old ink residues.

Gsm

An acronym that stands for grams per square metre. The higher the gsm number, the heavier the paper. This is a European measurement.

H

Halftone

A way of reproducing a continuous tone image in printed form. The image is split up into a system of dots that vary in size or in distance apart. When printed, the small dots, although printed in a single colour, black for example, fool the eye and brain into perceiving them as tones of grey. This also forms the basis of four-colour process printing, which gives the illusion of full colour.

HP

Stands for hot-pressed paper, one of the three most common paper surfaces. It is a literal term for paper that has been pressed between hot metal plates (or something similar) to make the surface very smooth.

I

Indirect stencil

A light-sensitive stencil film that is exposed, developed and applied to a damp mesh. This can also apply to a hand or mechanically cut version that is not light sensitive, but can be applied to a mesh in the same way (*see* also 'Capillary film').

Interference ink or pigment

Interference pigments consist of layers of metal oxide deposited on to mica. The resulting pigment refracts and reflects the light, scattering it through the various layers, hence the name 'interference'. Colours mixed with interference pigments appear to change depending upon the angle from which they are viewed.

L

Liquid crystal mesh

Screen meshes woven with hybrid super fibres. These are made of thermotropic (heat-reactive) liquid crystal polymer, crystallized at a specific temperature and stabilized after the spinning process. This results in a super-fine thread that gives a smooth mesh surface. These meshes are used in the electronics industry, where the highest possible resolutions and mesh tensions are desirable.

M

Mesh count

The number of threads per centimetre (in Europe) or per inch (in America) in screen fabric. The lower the number, the bigger the openings; the higher the number, the smaller they are. This controls the amount of ink that can pass through the mesh and therefore the amount deposited on the material underneath.

Mesh geometry

The combined effect of mesh count, weave type and thread diameter. It describes all of the aspects of mesh construction that will affect its performance in use.

Monofilament

A strand or fibre made of a solid, flexible material. In the case of screens, this is usually polyester.

Mould-made paper

Paper that is manufactured in a cylinder mould. Paper pulp is put into a vat that contains a rotating cylinder covered in a wire mesh. The cylinder is only partially submerged into the pulp. As the cylinder slowly rotates, the paper fibres collect on the mesh in matted form. The matted fibres are continuously taken off the cylinder as it reaches the top of its rotation in a process called couching, which means that the fibres are laid out flat on felts ready to transfer to another surface. They are then processed further to make rolls or cut sheets of paper.

Multi-filament

Threads made up of twisted or woven smaller strands.

N

Nitrile gloves

Sometimes called 'medical grade', nitrile gloves are made of synthetic rubber. Unlike latex gloves, they do not puncture so easily and can withstand a wider variety of chemicals than ordinary vinyl or latex gloves.

NOT

Referring to paper, it stands for 'not hot pressed'. This kind of paper has a matt, medium rough surface texture.

O

OHP film

Overhead-projection film with a special coating on one side that will accept inkjet ink from a digital printer. OHP film can be used to make positives for photo exposure, provided that the settings on the printer are set to print out the blackest possible image.

Overprint

Where one translucent colour layer prints over another to produce a third colour where they cross. Translucent magenta over cyan, for example, produces a purple overprint.

P

Photoemulsion

Liquid emulsion that has been sensitized to ultraviolet light coated on to screens with a coating trough, dried and exposed to form a photostencil.

Photostencil

A screen-print stencil that has been produced by exposing a black positive carried on a translucent support (such as a film positive) on to a screen that has been coated with a layer of light-sensitive emulsion. The emulsion hardens, or 'cures', in reaction to ultraviolet light. Where the emulsion was protected from the light by the black areas of the positive, the emulsion stays soft and soluble. The screen is washed and those areas wash away, leaving them open for the ink to pass through when printing.

Precise registration

A screen-printing table with precise registration has a vacuum bed held in place by springs. This type of bed can be moved in very small increments, so that the position of the paper can be adjusted very precisely after set-up.

Print-down frame

Another name for an exposure unit.

Printout

The name given to a digital print on paper or film, but also the waste screenprints that are the normal part of a printing run. The latter is usually kept in a print studio and recycled whenever it is needed for testing print quality, colour or general troubleshooting. It saves wasting good paper.

Q

Quad Crown

An imperial paper or poster measurement (30 × 40in) that has survived European metrification. The size of the print bed on a screen-printing table is still often referred to as being Double (20 × 30in) or Quad Crown, for example.

R

Reclaiming

Refers to reusing a screen, that is, removing the old stencil with a stencil remover and sometimes also ink residues with a caustic paste or liquid.

Reducing base

See 'Extender base'.

Registration

Aligning one layer of printed colour with the next, throughout the print, so that they fit together correctly to create the image.

Resolution

In digital terms, the resolution is expressed by the number of dots per inch (dpi). Low numbers such as 72dpi represent low-resolution images that do not take up much space on the hard drive of a computer and are therefore 'small'. If such an image is enlarged, it will lose quality or 'resolution'. In analogue (particularly photographic) print terms, it means the sharpness or crispness of a print.

Retardant

A chemical additive that slows the drying time of printing inks. Useful in screenprinting to counter the tendency for ink to dry in the mesh.

Retensionable screens

See 'Dynamic screens'.

RIP

An acronym for 'raster image processing', computer software that translates page description language (for example, Post-script), using specific mathematical algorithms, into a form that the printer can read and output. A raster image is also known as a bitmap.

Rough paper

Rough paper has a very rough surface produced by using rough felts for couching (transferring the paper from one surface to another) when the paper is being made.

S

Scoop coater

Another name for a coating trough.

Screen

Can refer to the mesh-covered screen-printing frame and also to the system of dots that make up a halftone image.

Screen filler

Screen filler or screen block is a viscous liquid that is applied to the screen mesh with a small brush to spot out pinholes in a photographic stencil. It can also be used on its own to make a stencil by hand. There are varieties suitable for oil-based inks and for water-based inks. Those for use with oil-based ink can be washed out with water but are not suitable to make a stencil if water-based inks are being used. Those used to resist water-based ink need to be removed from the screen with stencil remover just like a photostencil.

Separations

The prepared layers of a print separated into colours.

Seriography

An American name for the screen-print process meant to distance the Fine Art, often hand-pulled, print from its more commercial counterparts.

Stochastic dots

A pseudo-random system of dots of the same size that are distributed sparsely or densely to simulate varying shades of grey in an image. Also used in four-colour separations.

Substrate

Anything that is being printed on, such as paper, fabric, metal, glass and so on.

Swirl marks

These are swirling marks that appear in the print when the screen is not snapping off the paper quickly enough as the squeegee passes over it to pull the print. They are often more noticeable in translucent colours. The solution is to slightly raise the frame that holds the screen. Contributing factors can also be that the ink is too thick and tacky, or a vacuum is not working properly and is not holding the paper down successfully.

T

Thixotropic ink

An ink with a gel-like texture, which, when stirred or shaken, becomes liquid and then returns to its gel-like state.

Trapping

Adding an overlap to some of the colour layers to avoid or mask slight misregistrations (*see* also 'Bleed').

V

Vector files

In computer-generated images, vector files are created using points, lines, curves or shapes based on mathematical models. Vectors are also called 'paths', which lead from one point or node to another to describe a shape. Adobe Illustrator is a vector-based programme.

W

Washout

When the exposed photostencil is washed to remove the uncured emulsion that has not been exposed to the light.

Washout booth/trough

A piece of equipment in which to wash out screens and also to reclaim them. Often it will have a light panel, so that you can see through the screen to make sure that it is clear and/or clean.

LIST OF SUPPLIERS

www.adcolour.co.uk (adcolour-education.co.uk) ink/screens/equipment

www.amrpress.co.uk specialist printmaking equipment/equipment removals

www.apfitzpatrick.co.uk suppliers of Lascaux inks and media

www.art-equipment.co.uk equipment manufacturers

www.atlantisart.co.uk general art supplies/screen supplies

www.bookbinding.co.uk (Shepherds) fine art papers/bookbinding supplies

www.cassart.co.uk general art supplies/printmaking supplies

www.cornelissen.com pigments

www.daveroper.co.uk inks/screens/equipment

www.greatart.co.uk online general art supplies

www.handprinted.co.uk inks/screens/emulsions/craft supplies

www.harryrochat.com intaglio relief, but also second-hand equipment

www.hawthorneprintmaker.com printmaking supplies

www.huntthemoon.co.uk specialist screen-printing supplies

www.jacksonsart.com general art supplies/printmaking supplies

www.johnpurcell.net printmaking papers/TW graphics inks

www.lawrence.co.uk general art supplies/printmaking supplies

www.londongraphics.co.uk general art supplies/printmaking supplies

www.natgraph.co.uk equipment manufacturers

www.peterpotter.co.uk equipment manufacturers

www.rkburt.com fine paper and digital supplies

www.robco.co.uk (Roberson and Co) artists supplies/pigments and metallics

www.seawhite.co.uk general art materials/paper/inks

www.screencoloursystems.co.uk inks/screens/screen-recovering service/emulsions

www.screenstretch.co.uk inks/screens/screen-recovering service/emulsions

www.silkscreeningprintsupplies.co.uk inks/emulsions/screens equipment

www.turnersart.co.uk general art supplies/inks/screens/equipment/emulsions

www.wickedprintingstuff.com inks/screens/equipment

List of printmaking studios and workshops in England, Scotland and Ireland that offer access and courses. Some also have galleries and sell supplies (not exclusive to screenprinting).

www.arthub.org.uk (London)

www.artichokeprintmaking.com (London)

www.atelier-ji.com (London)

www.bathartistprintmakers.co.uk (Bath)

www.bip-art.co.uk (Brighton)

www.birminghamprintmakers.org (Birmingham)

www.bpw.org.uk (Belfast print workshop)

www.corkprintmakers.ie (Cork)

www.dca.org.uk (Dundee)

www.doubleelephant.org.uk (Exeter)

www.eastlondonprintmakers.co.uk (London)

www.edinburghprintmakers.co.uk (Edinburgh)

www.gainsborough.org (Sudbury)

www.gpchq.org.uk (Stroud)

www.graphicstudiodublin.com (Dublin)

www.heatherleys.org (London)

www.hotbedpress.org (Salford)

www.inkspotpress.co.uk (Brighton)

www.johnhowardprintstudios.com (Cornwall)

www.leicesterprintworkshop.com (Leicester)

www.londonprintstudio.org.uk (London)

www.northernprint.org.uk (Newcastle-upon-Tyne)

www.northstarstudio.wordpress.com (Brighton)

www.ochreprintstudio.co.uk (Guildford)

www.oxfordprintmakers.co.uk (Oxford)

www.peackockvisualarts.com (Aberdeen)

www.pellafort-press.co.uk (London)

www.pooleprintmakers.org.uk (Poole)

www.printmarketproject.com (Cardiff)

www.redhotpress.org.uk (Southampton)

www.regionalprintcentre.ac.uk (Wrexham)

www.seacourt-ni.org.uk (Bangor, N. Ireland)

www.slaughterhaus.net (London)

www.spikeprintstudio.org (Bristol)

www.stbarnabuspress.co.uk (Cambridge)

www.thamesbarrier-printstudio.wordpress.com (London)

www.thebluecoat.org.uk (Liverpool)

www.thecurwenstudio.co.uk (Middlesex)

www.theprintblock.com (Whitstable)

www.theprintshed.net (Hereford)

www.volcaniceditions.com (Brighton)

www.wypw.org (Yorkshire)

INDEX

Related Titles From Crowood

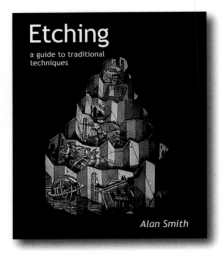

Etching

ALAN SMITH

ISBN 978 1 86126 597 5

160pp, 200 illustrations

Fine Art Screenprinting

MAGGIE JENNINGS

ISBN 978 1 84797 981 0

144pp, 290 illustrations

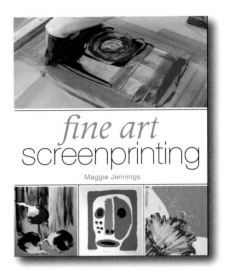

Linocut for Artists and Designers

NICK MORLEY

ISBN 978 1 78500 145 1

176pp, 300 illustrations

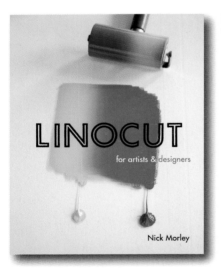

Making Woodblock Prints

MERLYN CHESTERMAN AND
ROD NELSON

ISBN 978 1 84797 903 2

112pp, 160 illustrations

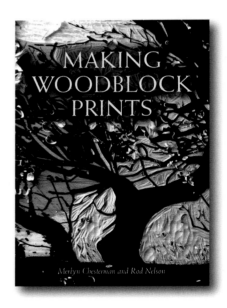

In case of difficulty in ordering, contact the Sales Office:

The Crowood Press Ltd
Ramsbury
Wiltshire
SN8 2HR
UK

Tel: 44 (0) 1672 520320
enquiries@crowood.com

www.crowood.com